# BRITISH POLIT[...]
# IN THE 1930s AND 1940s

Stock check
2007

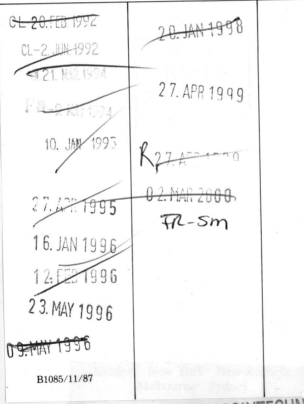

Published by the Press Syndicate of the University of Cambridge
The Pitt Building, Trumpington Street, Cambridge CB2 1RP
32 East 57th Street, New York, NY 10022, USA
10 Stamford Road, Oakleigh, Melbourne 3166, Australia

© Cambridge University Press 1987

First published 1987

Printed in Great Britain at the University Press, Cambridge

*British Library cataloguing in publication data*

Adelman, Paul
  British politics in the 1930s and 1940s.
  – (Cambridge topics in history)
  1. Great Britain – Politics and government – 20th century
  I. Title
  320.941   HN231

ISBN 0 521 31729 0

SE

# Contents

# Acknowledgements

The author and publisher would like to thank the following for permission to reproduce extracts and illustrations:

1.1 Emanuel Shinwell, *Conflict without Malice*, Odhams, 1955, p. 113; 1.2, 1.12 *The Diary of Beatrice Webb*, vol. iv, ed. Norman and Jeanne MacKenzie, published by Virago Press Ltd, 1985, in association with The London School of Economics and Political Science. © The London School of Economics and Political Science; 1.3 Sir Oswald Mosley, *My Life*, Sanctuary Press Ltd; 1.4 Robert Skidelsky, *Politics and the Slump*, Macmillan, London and Basingstoke; 1.5 David Low cartoon, *Evening Standard*, 1930; supplied by permission of *The Standard*; 1.6, 1.10, 1.11 The Times Newspapers Limited copyright – 1.8.1931, 28.8.1931, 29.10,1931; 1.7, 1.9 David Marquand, *Ramsay MacDonald*, Cape, 1977; 1.8 Cabinet Minutes 46 (31), CAB 23/67, reproduced with the permission of the Controller of Her Majesty's Stationery Office; 2.1, 2.5 Harold Macmillan, *The Winds of Change 1914–39*, Macmillan, London and Basingstoke, 1966; 2.2 Strube cartoon, *Daily Express*, 1926, supplied by permission of *The Standard*; 2.3 'Safety First' poster, 1929, Conservative Party Archives; 2.4, 2.9, 2.10 R. R. James (ed.), *Chips: the Diaries of Sir Henry Channon*, George Weidenfeld and Nicolson Ltd, 1967; 2.6 Viscount Templewood, *Nine Troubled Years*, Collins, 1954; 2.7 Nigel Nicolson (ed.), *Harold Nicolson's Diaries and Letters 1930–39*, 1966; 2.8 'Still Hope', reproduced by permission of *Punch*; 3.1 F. W. S. Craig, *British General Election Manifestos 1918–66*, Parliamentary Research Services, Chichester, 1970; 3.2 Pat Sloan (ed.), *John Cornford: a memoir*, Cape, 1938, courtesy of the estate of Pat Sloan; 3.3 Robin Skelton, *Poetry of the Thirties*, Cape, courtesy of the estate of Pat Sloan; illustration p.57, Communist Party Library; 3.4 Oswald Mosley, *The Greater Britain*, 1932, Sanctuary Press Ltd; 3.5 Sir Oswald Mosley, *My Life*, Sanctuary Press Ltd; 3.6 Philip Toynbee, *Friends Apart*, Macgibbon and Kee, 1954, Grafton Books, a division of the Collins Publishing Group; 3.7 Fenner Brockway, *Inside the Left*, Allen and Unwin, 1942; 4.1, 4.2 F. W. S. Craig, *British General Election Manifestos 1918–66*, Parliamentary Research Services, Chichester, 1970; 4.3 Harold Macmillan, *Tides of Fortune 1945–1955*, Macmillan, London and Basingstoke, 1969; 4.4 *The Collected Essays, Journalism and Letters of George Orwell*, courtesy of the estate of the late Sonia Brownell Orwell and Secker and Warburg Ltd; 4.5 Hugh Dalton, *The Fateful Years: Memoirs 1931–45*, Muller, Blond and White Ltd, 1957; 4.6 J. B. Priestley, *Postscripts*, reprinted by permission of William Heinemann Ltd, 1940; 4.7 J. T. Murphy, *Labour's Big Three*, 1948, reprinted by permission of The Bodley Head; 5.1, 5.7 Douglas Jay, *Change and Fortune*, Hutchinson, 1980; 5.2 Kenneth Harris, *Attlee*, George Weidenfeld and Nicolson Ltd, 1982; 5.3 Francis Williams, *A Prime Minister Remembers*, reprinted by permission of William Heinemann Ltd, 1961; 5.4 C. R. Attlee, *As it Happened*, reprinted by permission of William Heinemann Ltd, 1954; 5.5 Vicky cartoon, await claim; 5.6 Philip M. Williams (ed.), *The Diary of Hugh Gaitskell 1945–56*, Cape, 1983; 6.1 Lloyd George, *War Memoirs*, Odhams; 6.2 Charles Eade (ed.) *Churchill: by his Contemporaries*, Hutchinson, 1953; 6.3 Randolph S. Churchill (ed.), *Into Battle: Speeches by the Right Hon. Winston Churchill*, reprinted by kind permission of Curtis Brown Ltd, on behalf of the Estate of Sir Winston Churchill, copyright Estate of Sir Winston Churchill; 6.4 Winston S. Churchill, *The Second World War*, vol. 1, 'The Gathering Storm', Cassell Ltd, 1948; 6.5 R. R. James (ed.), *Chips: The Diaries of Sir Henry Channon*, George Weidenfeld and Nicolson Ltd, 1967; 6.6 *The Art of the Possible: the Memoirs of Lord Butler*, Penguin Books, 1973.

*Cover illustration*: 'Our New Defence' by David Low, *Evening Standard* 4 October 1938; cartoon supplied by permission of *The Standard*. Low's commentary on the Munich Settlement, 1938, shows Neville Chamberlain and Halifax, led by Sir John Simon, playing with the innocent lambs, while Beaverbrook rejoices on the right.

# Introduction: British politics in the 1930s and 1940s

## A Introduction

The outstanding themes in British political history from the end of the first World War until 1929, are undoubtedly the growth of the Labour Party and the decline of the Liberal Party. The causes of this process are complex and controversial. Some historians stress political factors: the split in the Liberal Party after 1916, for example, or the impact of the fourth Reform Act of 1918. Other historians emphasise long-term social and economic factors: the effects of rapid social change and worsening economic conditions on the working class, and the rise of a mass trades union movement closely linked with the Labour Party.

In the short-run, a key factor was the leadership of Ramsay MacDonald and the strategy he adopted towards the Liberal Party. For MacDonald, the key to Labour advance in the 1920s lay in the destruction of the Liberal Party as an alternative party of government on the Left. His policy succeeded brilliantly. In the general election of 1924, following the collapse of the first Labour government, the Liberals were reduced to forty MPs in the House of Commons, and had been pushed permanently into third place in the electoral stakes. Even the leadership, money and spectacular economic plans of Lloyd George in the 1929 election could not give the Liberal Party more than 59 seats compared with Labour's 288.

By contrast with Labour and the Liberals, there were no fundamental changes in the national position of the Conservative Party after the First World War. The Tories possessed a secure electoral base among the middle classes – including women over the age of thirty who were now enfranchised – and an important section of the working class. But they also gained in the 1920s from the fragmentation and dissipation of the 'radical' vote as a result of the rivalry between Labour and Liberal – a process which was helped by the persuasive tactics and policies of Stanley Baldwin [2.1]. Hence, despite the democratisation of the British electoral system after 1918, the Conservative Party was still able to win overall majorities in the general elections of 1922 and 1924. This achievement was, as yet, beyond the strength of the Labour Party and, even more, the Liberals.

The major political developments in the 1920s continued into the period between 1929 and 1951, and were, if anything, strengthened. For at the beginning of the 1930s Britain still possessed a three-party system. The Liberal Party might be a party in decline, but in terms of voting power, prestige and leadership, it was still an integral part of the British political system. Though it only obtained fifty-nine seats in the general election of 1929, it did poll some five million votes. The part played by Sir Herbert Samuel, acting leader of the Liberal Party during the illness of Lloyd George, in the formation of the National government in the summer of 1931, was a vital one. Partly as a result of his labours, both he and his fellow-Liberal, Lord Reading, were rewarded with important Cabinet posts. Even the position of Lloyd George, though he remained outside the National government, was a formidable one. By contrast, at the end of this period after the general election of 1951, the Liberals polled less than one million votes and ended up with only six MPs; their leaders were obscure men largely unknown to the British public. By that date the Liberal Party, squeezed between the big battalions of Socialists and Tories, seemed to have been eliminated as a serious force in British politics, and the country appeared to have returned to a real two-party system.

This fact in itself underlines once again the continuous advance of the Labour Party. For the remarkable expansion of the Labour vote in the 1920s – from just over four million in 1922 to over eight million in 1929 – was temporarily halted but not checked in the disastrous general election of 1931 [1.11]. Indeed the decline of the Labour Party in the 1930s was more apparent than real. It still possessed a solid bedrock of votes among the industrial working class upon which it could build [1.12]; it clearly possessed the capacity to govern; and the special circumstances which had helped the Conservatives after 1931 were bound to pass away. That the Labour Party would eventually gain an overall electoral majority seemed certain: that it won a landslide majority in the general election of 1945 may be attributed mainly to the special experience of war-time [4.3, 4.4 and 4.5].

In some ways, however, it is the staying power of the Conservatives which is most remarkable during this whole period. It is understandable that they gained from the 'National' appeal in the 1930s, though, in stark contrast to what happened during the First World War, the continuation of this appeal by the Churchill Coalition government ultimately benefited the Left rather than the Right. But the swift adaptation of the Conservative Party after 1945 to the harsh realities of a new age, was a significant achievement, especially as the party was led by Churchill, a man who was basically out of tune with contemporary developments [6.6]. After the general election of 1951 the Conservative Party was poised on the brink of thirteen years of power: a change in political fortunes that would have seemed astonishing to most observers at the end of July 1945.

## B   The politics of the National government (1931–40)

The origin of the National government lies in the financial crisis of August

1931 [**1.6, 1.7 and 1.8**]. It was during this major crisis that Ramsay MacDonald failed to carry his Labour Cabinet with him in the programme of government cuts – especially cuts in unemployment benefits – which he and the other party leaders believed were necessary to achieve financial stability. The idea of a *National* government, a coalition of Conservatives, Liberals and some Labour MPs to deal temporarily with these complex problems, seems to have originated with Liberal MP, Sir Herbert Samuel, though it soon received strong support from King George V.

Politically, there were strong reasons why Samuel should support such a move. A National government would give the Liberals the chance of office once again, and help to paper over the cracks which had appeared in the Parliamentary Party over what attitude it should adopt towards the second Labour government. MacDonald's reasons were more complex. Though he was loath to break with his party, in the end his sense of 'duty', reinforced by the pleas of the King, made him decide to carry on as Prime Minister and appeal for support to his ex-colleagues in the Labour government [**1.9**]. In the end only three members, Snowden, Sankey, and Thomas agreed to follow him. All four were soon afterwards expelled from the Labour Party. The attitude of the Conservative leaders was more equivocal. Their party had been winning by-elections since 1930, and they could reasonably expect to win the next election whenever it came. Nevertheless, for Baldwin especially, there was much to be said for supporting a National government. The 'National' appeal suited him perfectly at this time on both personal and public grounds. He could use it, buttressed by Liberal ministers and a Labour Prime Minister, to frustrate the right-wing Tory opposition to his own leadership which had been growing since 1929, and to bring the party back to that centrist conciliatory position which he had advanced in the 1920s [**2.1**].

The small Cabinet of ten members formed by MacDonald was necessarily dominated by Liberals and Conservatives. The three Labour ex-ministers, Snowden, Thomas, and Sankey, were appointed Chancellor of the Exchequer, Dominions Secretary, and Lord Chancellor, respectively. Baldwin became Lord President, and his fellow-Tories, Neville Chamberlain, Cunliffe-Lister and Hoare, went to the Ministry of Health, the Board of Trade, and the India Office. Samuel obtained the Home Office, and his fellow-Liberal, the Marquess of Reading, the Foreign Office. Two outstanding politicians were excluded: Lloyd George, who (to the relief of MacDonald and Baldwin) was seriously ill during the events of August, and Winston Churchill, who had now reinforced his reputation (in Baldwin's phrase) as 'a disruptive influence', by leading a public campaign against political reforms in India in defiance of the Conservative leadership. Once the major financial decisions had been taken by the new government – including the full package of cuts, and the abandonment of the Gold Standard on 21 September 1931 – MacDonald, to the consternation of the Liberals, yielded to Tory pressure and agreed to an early general election to restore national unity and confidence.

The election of October 1931 was a triumph for the Conservatives, a disaster for Labour, and a humiliation for the Liberals [1.11]. The Conservatives won 473 seats; Labour was reduced to 52 seats; and though the Liberals had 72 MPs they were now hopelessly divided. They had split more or less equally between the Simonites (led by John Simon and virtually indistinguishable from the Tories) and the Samuelites, together with the minuscule family group of four led by Lloyd George, who had now broken with the official Liberal party. Inevitably the Conservatives increased their hold on the government. They had eleven out of the twenty seats in the new enlarged Cabinet, and Neville Chamberlain, *the* outstanding Tory minister, now replaced Snowden as Chancellor of the Exchequer. Furthermore, with the government's adoption of Protection in 1932 (a policy of fostering home produce and manufacture by import duties), the Samuelite Liberal Ministers retired to the Opposition benches. This left MacDonald even more isolated. The Prime Minister still exerted some personal authority, particularly over foreign affairs, but politically his position was now an impossible one. In June 1935 he was edged out as Prime Minister by Baldwin, who shortly afterwards won a decisive electoral victory, due more perhaps to economic revival than the defence issues on which attention has been focused.

Though, in personnel, the National government became more obviously Conservative under Baldwin, and even more so after Chamberlain became Premier in 1937, the 'National' label was not entirely cosmetic during these years. Both in 1931 and 1935 it helped to win over Liberal and floating voters, something which the Tories could not so easily have done by themselves. National Labour men and National Liberals like Simon and Thomas remained members of the government; Malcolm MacDonald (Ramsay's son) became Colonial Secretary; and younger progressive Tories, such as Anthony Eden and Stanley, were promoted by Baldwin. In terms of policy, the influence of Baldwin's so-called 'New Conservatism' is even stronger. The Conservative leader's support for political reform in India marks in some ways a turning-point in Tory attitudes towards the Empire; while, after the restoration of the cuts in 1934, the government's social policies were reasonably humane. Similarly, its more pragmatic financial outlook did much, indirectly, to encourage the economic revival of the later thirties.

Baldwin went out in a blaze of glory in May 1937 after his skilful handling of the Abdication Crisis in the previous year, an episode in which he again found himself on the opposite side to Churchill. Under his successor, Chamberlain, it was foreign policy more than anything else that produced tensions within the National government [2.7]. Winston Churchill, who certainly resented his exclusion from office after 1935, became the leading Conservative opponent of Appeasement during Chamberlain's premiership. He was joined by Eden (after Eden's resignation over the issue in February 1938) and by Duff Cooper (after the Munich agreement), by which time the Conservative anti-Appeasers numbered about thirty MPs. Yet what is remarkable at this time is the ineffectiveness of these anti-Appeasers, and how loyal the Conservative Party, both in parliament and in the country, was to Chamberlain and his policies [2.10]. This remained true until the German attack on Poland on 1 September 1939 signalled the collapse of the policy of Appeasement, and with it, within a year, the end of the National government itself.

## C  The Labour Party in the 1930s

The events of August to November 1931 marked a profound turning-point in the history of the Labour Party. Its old leaders had gone; after the October election the Parliamentary Party was reduced to fifty-two MPs (lower than in 1918!); almost all the ex-ministers had lost their seats; its organisation was in disarray; and it lacked even the semblance of a positive programme to offer the electorate [1.12].

The first need for the Labour Party after these crises was to resolve the problem of leadership. Arthur Henderson acted as a stop-gap until George Lansbury, the senior ex-minister to survive the election, took over as leader in 1932, with Clement Attlee as his deputy. But though Lansbury was respected by the whole Labour movement, he was now over seventy, and, as a life-long pacifist, it was difficult for him to act as a convincing spokesman for the party when defence and foreign policy issues were rapidly coming to the fore. After his brutal mauling by Ernest Bevin at the Party Conference in October 1935, Lansbury resigned. Attlee became temporary leader until after the general election a month or so later. One result of that election was the return to parliament of most of the ex-Labour ministers. Attlee was therefore opposed by Herbert Morrison and Arthur Greenwood in the subsequent leadership contest, but was successfully elected [5.1]. One reason for this was the strong support he received from Bevin and the great trade unions, and this in itself reflects the greater importance of the TUC within the Labour Party after 1931.

Another consequence of 1931 was a more realistic attitude by the new Labour leadership to the problems of government. What was now needed, they believed, was the formulation of detailed practical policies *before* Labour again took office, as blueprints for legislation. Here the main work was done by the Policy Sub-Committee of the National Executive, where men like Herbert Morrison and Hugh Dalton were able to produce plans on topics such as banking, transport, coal and social services. These plans became the basis for Labour's published programmes, *For Socialism and Peace* (1935), *Labour's Immediate Programme* (1937) and, ultimately, the domestic legislation of the post-war Labour governments.

As always, one of the fundamental problems facing Labour was that of party unity, and this became inextricably linked with the menacing issues of war and peace. After the disaffiliation of the Independent Labour Party (ILP) in 1932, some of its members remained within the Labour Party and, in collaboration with other left-wingers and pacifists, formed the Socialist League, whose dominating figure became Sir Stafford Cripps. The influence of the League was seen particularly in the field of foreign policy and defence. Its supporters were strongly committed to 'peace and disarmament', and were even critical of the credentials of the League of Nations – 'an international Burglars' Union', in Cripps's famous phrase. Labour's right-wing was just as belligerent. Led by Hugh Dalton and Ernest Bevin, it supported a policy of 'collective security' through a strong League of Nations, and was prepared to use force against an aggressor, thus accepting, implicitly, the need for British rearmament.

The clash between Labour Left and Right was displayed at the 1935 Labour Party Conference. The resignation of Lansbury that followed, marked a real defeat for pacifism within the party. But the 'hard' Left remained unaffected. Indeed, in some ways its position was strengthened in 1936 owing to the pusillanimity of the government over Italian and German expansion and, even more, the extraordinary emotional appeal of the Spanish Republican cause to the entire Labour movement. This gave a great propaganda boost to the British Left generally, helped and symbolised by the foundation that year of the 'Left Book Club', and later, the weekly *Tribune*, financed by Cripps. All this culminated at the end of 1936 in a 'Unity Campaign', organised by the Socialist League in collaboration with the ILP and the Communist Party 'to unite all sections of the working class movement . . . in common struggle against Fascism, Reaction and War'. The Labour Party Executive firmly opposed the Campaign, and it was wound up at the beginning of 1937, followed a few months later by the voluntary dissolution of the Socialist League.

This was a victory for the Right. By that time too, encouraged by Dalton and Bevin, and alarmed at the growing tide of aggression, feeling within the Labour Party generally was beginning to move against its rigid anti-rearmament stance. In 1937 the Parliamentary Labour Party (PLP) decided to abstain rather than vote against the Services' estimates, and the Party Conference that year in effect supported the government's rearmament measures. The Left, however, remained adamant in its opposition, and at the end of 1938 Cripps made one final effort to achieve an anti-government union of the Left through the 'Popular Front' movement. It met the same reaction from the Labour Party leadership as before. This time, however, Cripps and his two chief supporters, George Strauss and Aneurin Bevan, were expelled from the party – a move that was strongly supported by a special Party Conference. Characteristically, Cripps, unlike his two fellow-rebels, remained outside the Labour Party until 1945.

It seems difficult to deny that disunity within the Labour Party damaged it electorally in the 1930s. Though the party made up some lost ground after 1931, at local rather than national level, the results of the 1935 general election were a bitter disappointment. The party did win back about a hundred seats, and its leading figures returned to the House of Commons; but with 432 MPs, the National government still retained an enormous majority. Nor was this verdict unexpected. Economic revival was clearly under way by 1935, and by committing his party to 'collective security' and moderate rearmament, Baldwin cut the ground from under the feet of the Labour Party. Nor was Attlee any match for Baldwin in terms of popular appeal. What all this meant was that the Liberal and floating vote was still loyal to the government. And this remained true up to 1939. By 1945 of course the situation was quite different. Ironically, therefore, it was war rather than peace, that proved the electoral salvation of the Labour Party.

## D British politics in the Second World War

Once war was declared on 3 September 1939, an 'electoral truce' was agreed upon by the three main political parties, which meant in practice that they would not fight one another at by-elections. Since Labour was not prepared to join the government, owing to its distrust of Chamberlain, the Prime Minister was forced to strengthen his team by the inclusion of the leading Conservative dissidents, Churchill (who returned to the Admiralty) and Eden. The appointment of Churchill was particularly significant. Though he remained personally loyal to Chamberlain until the bitter end, his energy, confidence and past political record meant that he was, in effect, an alternative Prime Minister. Nevertheless, even the inclusion of Churchill and Eden did not fundamentally change the character of the ministry. It was still dominated by Chamberlain and his henchmen – Halifax, Hoare, Simon and Wood. Perhaps it was this that helps to account for the inability of the government to provide either inspiration or effective mobilisation of the nation's resources during the period of the 'phoney war', the period 1939–40, characterised by Allied and German inactivity on the Western Front. As A. J. P. Taylor suggests, 'The government were still moving into war backwards with their eyes tightly closed'.

The anxiety which the Labour Opposition and many Conservatives felt at the lack-lustre war leadership of Chamberlain came to a head in the spring of 1940, following the ignominious withdrawal of the British forces from Norway. In the remarkable debate that followed in the House of Commons on 7–8 May, the government's majority slumped from well over 200 to 81, and it was clear that the Prime Minister had lost the confidence of an important section of his party [2.10]. On 9 May Chamberlain reluctantly accepted that a National government was inevitable, and, since the Labour Party refused to serve under him, it was obvious that he would have to resign. Who should succeed him? The choice lay between Churchill and Halifax – either of whom was acceptable to the Labour Party. On the evening of 10 May 1940, Churchill became Prime Minister, primarily because he wanted the job more fiercely than Halifax [6.4].

The original War Cabinet formed by Churchill was a small one of five members, although it was later enlarged. It included two Labour men, Attlee and Greenwood, and two Conservatives apart from himself, Chamberlain and Halifax. Leading Labour men like Alexander, Bevin, Morrison and Dalton (and one or two Liberals) received important government posts. Even so, Labour had only sixteen places in the new Coalition government compared with the Tories' fifty-two, and the majority of these had served under Chamberlain. Most of the members of the Conservative anti-Appeasement group were ill-served in the allocation of places. For Churchill, this was a recognition of political necessity. Chamberlain was personally popular with the Parliamentary Conservative Party, many of whose members had long-standing grievances against the new Prime Minister. Nor did Churchill wish to create further divisions within his party. His political position was strengthened, however, when, after Chamberlain's retirement in October and death in November 1940, he became official leader of the Conservative Party, thus attracting to himself the instinctive Tory reactions of loyalty and deference. Not that this, or indeed his parliamentary position, was really the basis of his war-time power. His strength lay in his command of a truly National government, and his indispensable role as war leader, expressing and symbolising the popular opposition to Nazi Germany and its allies.

This meant that Churchill, within the general parameters of the political alliance, could organise his government as he wished. There was still no wholesale proscription of the 'men of Munich' after Dunkirk, despite the virulent campaign conducted against them by some sections of the Press. Eden replaced Halifax as Foreign Secretary; Kingsley Wood was dropped from the War Cabinet – but so, later, was Arthur Greenwood, the Labour deputy leader, who had proved to be a hopeless minister. Indeed, as far as membership of the War Cabinet was concerned, Churchill was moved not by personal animosities, but by his own – occasionally eccentric – notions of competence and efficiency. Thus Bevin, Minister of Labour, Morrison,

Home Secretary, and later Cripps, were promoted to the War Cabinet. But so were friends or outsiders like Lords Beaverbrook and Woolton, generally to perform special tasks.

The events of 8–10 May 1940, when Churchill took over as leader of the War Cabinet, mark the one great political crisis of the war. After that date the government was never in any real danger, even in the dark days of the winter of 1942 when individual MPs like Emanuel Shinwell, Lord Winterton and Aneurin Bevan had plenty of material with which to attack the government's military incapacity [6.5]. But they had nothing positive to offer. And when, after the autumn of 1942 the tide began to turn in favour of the Allies, Churchill's personal position and that of the government were politically unassailable. Indeed, whereas the power of the House of Commons inevitably declined during the years of Churchill's war-time government, the strength and cohesion of the inner Cabinet grew – to some extent at the expense of and in opposition to the parliamentary parties. This was a situation that was to cause some difficulties, for the Labour Party especially, in the last years of the war.

As Minister of Defence as well as Prime Minister, Churchill was personally responsible for planning and waging war – a task that he accepted with relish. But his concentration on 'Grand Strategy' and his evident lack of interest in domestic issues did mean that it was Labour rather than the Conservatives who became identified with Reform and Reconstruction and appeared to be in closer touch with the aspirations of ordinary people. Labour both encouraged and gained from the left-ward trend in opinion which developed after 1940 and which was evident in much war-time propaganda and the new questioning mood of the public [4.6]. It also emerged, for example, in the foundation of the Commonwealth Party by the Christian Socialist, Sir Richard Acland, which won two by-elections in safe Conservative seats after 1942 – a harbinger of what was to come.

Some social reform *was* passed by the government during the war, and various commitments were entered into; for example over the social services and full employment. But it was Labour rather than the Conservatives who became identified with plans for post-war social and economic reform. This came out in the famous debate on the Beveridge Report in February 1943, when virtually the whole of the Parliamentary Labour Party voted against the government, the only occasion when it did so throughout the war. It was the Labour Party's suspicion of the social attitudes of Churchill and the right-wing Conservatives surrounding him, like Beaverbrook and Bracken, that convinced it, as the armies of the Allies pushed across Europe in 1944–5, that the Coalition should be brought to an end as soon as possible. It was this view, impressed upon Attlee by the 1945 Labour Party Conference, that helped to bring about the collapse of the Churchill Coalition government a few months later. Many Conservative MPs also welcomed an early return to party politics at this time, confident that behind the banner of Churchill they were bound to achieve an electoral victory. They were to be sadly disillusioned when the results began to appear on 26 July!

## E   The Labour governments 1945–51

The Parliamentary Labour Party which emerged as a result of the electoral victory of July 1945, was in many ways a new party. Out of the 393 Labour MPs in the House of Commons, about two-thirds were new and youngish members, and the majority were now middle-class professional people, unlike the old trades-union-dominated party of the 1930s. If the members of the PLP were new and young, this was not reflected in the Labour government. The leading ministers were the veterans of the movement, who had held high office during the war [4.7]. This was particularly true of the 'Big Three' – Attlee, Morrison and Bevin, who, together with Dalton and Cripps, formed the inner circle of power within the Cabinet. As a whole the Attlee government represented every important section of the Labour movement. It was this that helped to give it its unique unity and strength, and the loyal support of every major institution within the Labour Party.

The British people faced a grim prospect after 1945 owing to the depredations of the war. An American loan had to be quickly negotiated to carry the country through its immediate financial problems. Nevertheless, the government pushed ahead vigorously with its programme of nationalisation. The Bank of England was the first to be dealt with. This was followed by the nationalisation of civil aviation (1946); coal, and cable and wireless (1947); transport and electricity (1948); gas (1949). The pattern of organisation adopted for the new nationalised industries was that of the 'public corporation', which meant administration by semi-independent boards. The major reasons for this seem to have been the lack of any available alternative, and the strong commitment of Morrison, who was in charge of the nationalisation programme, to the 'public corporation' ideal. None of this part of the government's programme met anything but token resistance from the Opposition. This was partly because almost all the proposals concerned public utilities, where state and/or local enterprise had always played a significant role. This was not the case with their plans for the nationalisation of iron and steel. Here they were entering the field of manufacturing industry, and one which even the supporters of nationalisation accepted had a good record in terms of production and industrial relations. The Conservatives were therefore vigorous in their opposition, and even the Cabinet was divided over the wisdom of proceeding. In the end the Bill was postponed until 1949, and as the result of a deal with the House of Lords it only came into effect in 1951, on the eve of the Tory electoral victory!

During these early years, Labour also passed the major part of its social welfare legislation. James Griffiths was responsible for the National Insurance Act of 1946, which applied the basic principles laid down in the Beveridge Report (1942), and was therefore unopposed by the Conservatives. The story of the National Health Service Act, passed in the same year, was very different. Aneurin Bevan's Bill was a much more radical measure. It went considerably further in the direction of a truly *national* health service than any proposals made during the war, mainly in its insistence on the nationalisation of the hospitals. It was bitterly opposed by the leaders of the British Medical Association (tacitly supported by the Tories), mainly because they were fearful of doctors becoming full-time salaried servants of the state. It took all Bevan's charm and skill as a negotiator to overcome their resistance and get the National Health Service started in 1948.

British foreign policy between 1945 and 1950 was dominated by the formidable personality of Ernest Bevin. Soon after assuming office, Bevin came to feel that the major obstacle to European stability and good relations between the powers was the pressure and intransigence of the Soviet Union, especially over Germany. British unease was increased by the growing Soviet domination of Eastern Europe. By 1946, an 'iron curtain' (in Churchill's famous phrase) had descended dividing East from West [5.4]. In Germany, by the Potsdam Agreement, the country had been divided up into zones administered by the Allies – Britain, France, the United States and the Soviet Union. Quarrels between the Soviet Union and the other Occupying Powers soon broke out over reparations, the refugee problem, and the deliberate sovietisation of Eastern Germany. The conclusion Bevin drew from this worsening situation was the need for closer co-operation, military and economic, between the Western democracies; and, even more vital, that the United States must be prepared to assume a more positive military role in the defence of Western Europe against Soviet pressure. By 1949 both these aims had been secured.

By 1946–7 the United States had herself begun to accept Bevin's assumptions. In March 1947 the President proclaimed the 'Truman Doctrine', promising economic aid to 'free peoples' and reflecting US hostility to Communism. A few months later the US Secretary of State put forward his plan for 'Marshall Aid' for Europe – a recovery programme financed by the US which encouraged a closer relation of European economies. This proposal was seized upon with alacrity by Bevin, who became the European statesman primarily responsible for its acceptance and organisation, especially as the Soviet bloc rejected it. A year later, in

March 1948, Britain, France and the Benelux countries signed the Brussels Treaty of mutual aid against aggression.

In Germany by this time relations between the Occupying Powers had gone from bad to worse. The fusing of the British and American zones had already taken place, and the introduction of a much-needed currency reform there was used by the Soviet Union as an excuse to initiate the 'Berlin Blockade' in June 1948 – really an attempt to force the Western Powers out of Berlin and to weaken their growing co-operation. The blockade was called off in May 1949, owing to the success of the Western air-lift. The results of the 'Berlin Blockade' were profound. In Germany it eventually led to the establishment of the West German state. Even more momentously, it made the United States add its weight to that of the signatories of the Brussels Treaty, and this culminated in the setting up of the North Atlantic Treaty Organisation (NATO) in April 1949, providing for mutual assistance against aggression in the North Atlantic. Thus within four years, the Americans had abandoned their isolationist mood and were now directly committed to the defence of Western Europe. Two years earlier, the British government had taken its own secret decision to finance the development of an atomic bomb. The 'cold war' was clearly under way.

There was little effective opposition to Bevin's foreign policy. The 'Keep Left' group, led by R. H. S. Crossman, Michael Foot and Ian Mikardo, in 1947 supported a 'socialist foreign policy', with the implication that Britain should act as a 'third force' in the world, between the Soviet bloc and the United States. But by 1949, owing to recent Soviet policy in Czechoslovakia and Berlin, even this tenuous opposition had fizzled out. More serious, widespread and cogent were the criticisms directed against Bevin's policy towards Palestine, where his insensitive approach exacerbated what was already an impossible situation. In the end Britain got the worst of all possible worlds. By withdrawing from Palestine in May 1948 without any plan for the future of the territory, Britain earned the enmity of both Jews and Arabs and the moral censure of world opinion. By contrast, Attlee's handling of the issue of Indian independence was a model of good sense.

Whatever the successes or failures of Bevin's policies abroad, something of a turning-point was reached in the internal history of the Attlee government in 1947. The dreadful winter of that year led to a fuel crisis, loss of industrial production and heavy unemployment. An economic crisis merged with a financial one in the summer, owing to the rapid exhaustion of the US loan and a run on sterling. Grumbles about his leadership and the lack of economic planning were shrewdly used by Attlee to spike the guns of his main critic, Sir Stafford Cripps, by making him an offer he could not refuse – promotion to the new post of Minister of

Economic Affairs. This was followed in the autumn by a reconstruction of the ministry, which led to the shunting of Emanuel Shinwell into a defence post, and the promotion of outstanding younger men like Harold Wilson and Hugh Gaitskell. The growing domination in the economic field – and within the government – of Cripps, was reinforced when he succeeded Dalton as Chancellor of the Exchequer in November 1947.

Thus began 'The Cripps Era', which lasted until the Chancellor's retirement through ill-health in 1950. It was marked by real economic recovery. This was due to Sir Stafford's policy of 'Austerity' – drastic cuts in imports, defence and capital expenditure, wage restraint, controls and planning – all helped by Marshall Aid. The result was enormous increases in production and exports, and full employment. The way was paved for the consumer boom of the 1950s.

Labour's period of power ended with the general elections of 1950 and 1951 [**5.6 and 5.7**]. Despite great achievements, by the end of the 1940s the middle classes, whose votes had helped Labour to power in 1945, were clearly tiring of austerity, controls and shortages. The Tory cry of 'Set the people free', had a seductive ring. Moreover, even to the faithful, the appeal of further nationalisation was clearly fading; while with the general acceptance of the principles of the Welfare State, the declining generation of older Labour leaders found it more and more difficult to know what to turn to next. All this was worsened by continuing financial problems and the impact of the Korean War. For the first time since the 1930s, there were once again in 1950–1 deep and growing differences over principles within the Labour Party – a situation that was to erupt into open warfare between the Left and Right of the party during the long years in Opposition up to 1964.

## F   The Conservative Party in the post-war world

The results of the 1945 general election were a bitter blow to the Conservative Party, most of whose members had expected a decisive verdict in their favour. On the eve of the poll Churchill himself had told King George VI that he forecasted a Tory majority of between thirty and eighty seats. As Churchill said afterwards, he was 'deeply distressed at the prospect of sinking from a national to a party leader'. With only 213 seats to Labour's 393, the 1945 verdict was the worst electoral disaster that had struck the Conservative Party since 1906. It brought to an end a period of Tory power which had virtually lasted – apart from brief periods in the 1920s – since the First World War. The Conservatives now had to accept the frustrations and re-learn the duties of being an effective Opposition party.

Churchill was determined to continue as Conservative leader, and he carried out his parliamentary duties in a reasonable manner. But especially on domestic matters, his heart was not really in it. He preferred to concentrate on great international issues in speeches aimed at world-wide audiences, where his experience and enormous prestige could have some effect. Churchill accepted, as did the bulk of the Conservative Party, that the magnitude of the recent electoral disaster implied the need for re-organisation and a re-formulation of Conservative policy. This gave a real opportunity to the Tory reformers, especially R. A. Butler, to bring the Conservative Party into touch with the realities of a Labour-dominated post-war Britain.

The Tory reformers had not been entirely helpless or voiceless during the war itself. Butler was of course responsible for the 1944 Education Act which was supposed to provide 'secondary education for all'. He and other progressive Conservatives, like Quintin Hogg, had also strongly supported the Beveridge Report and similar reforms proposed by the Coalition government. But for Churchill and the Tory hierarchy these were peripheral issues, to be left alone until the war was won. It was not until the aftermath of electoral defeat that the Tory reformers were given the blessing of the party leader and the rank-and-file.

In 1946 Churchill appointed Lord Woolton as Chairman of the Conservative Party (as 'Uncle Fred' he had been a popular war-time Food Minister). Woolton concentrated on building up membership and raising money on a wider scale at constituency level. He was remarkably successful. Party membership increased by well over a million from the end of the war to 1948, and an appeal for a one million pound Fund was enthusiastically subscribed. Much of the money was used to improve Conservative organisation, both at the Central Office and locally, by the appointment of more full-time party agents. What this meant was that by 1950 the Conservative Party's organisation, which had declined consider-ably during the war, was once again more professional and effective than the basically *ad hoc* model of the Labour Party. Woolton's work was complemented by the recommendations of the Committee on Party Organisation headed by Sir David Maxwell-Fyfe, which aimed at 'democratising' the selection of prospective parliamentary candidates by limiting personal contributions to party funds. This was largely a symbolic gesture: it had little effect in the long run on the general character of the Conservative Parliamentary Party.

The main figure in Conservative policy-making was Butler, who was made head of the revived Conservative Research Department after the war [6.6]. There he was helped by younger reformers like Enoch Powell and Iain Macleod, and was given strong backing by Harold Macmillan, and also Anthony Eden. The major outcome of Butler's work was the 'Industrial Charter' of 1947. This deliberately was not a detailed policy-making document, but a statement of broad general principles, written for the times, and for internal rather than external consumption. Yet its publication was important. It indicated that the Conservative Party was now committed to the Welfare State, the mixed economy, and full employment. But it also asserted that these aims were not incompatible with an emphasis on individual initiative, freedom from unnecessary controls and private enterprise. The acceptance of the 'Industrial Charter' by the party, with the tacit support of Churchill, meant that the Tory reformers were now in the ascendant intellectually; and indeed the onslaught on 'creeping socialism' by the Tory old guard was not even treated seriously. The 'Industrial Charter' was followed by other more specialist reports, all of which were incorporated in the 1949 party document *The Right Road for Britain*.

The relationship between the work of the Tory reformers and the results of the general elections of 1950 and 1951 is problematic [**5.6 and 5.7**]. Even the reformers were pessimistic about the party's chances of regaining power easily – a mood which was enhanced by Labour's excellent by-election record during its years of power. For the Conservative Party in general, the 1950 election was a disappointment. Even the majority obtained in 1951 could hardly be regarded as a clear breakthrough for Conservatism, given the state of the popular vote. Nevertheless, together the two elections did show a small but significant shift in allegiance by the middle classes away from Labour towards the Conservative Party. This was probably helped a little by the work of Tory reform – organisationally, if not in terms of ideas – even though the major factor was probably disillusionment with Labour rather than enthusiasm for the Conservatives. Whatever the causes, the Conservatives obtained a narrow but firm grasp on power in 1951, which was to last until 1964, confirmed and strengthened by major electoral triumphs in 1955 and 1959. It was the 1950s that saw the real victory of Tory reform in ideas and personnel.

## G  Sources and reading guide

One of the major primary sources for British politics in the 1930s and 1940s are the published memoirs, diaries and letters of the leading politicians and observers close to the political scene. Many of the most important ones are quoted in the chapters that follow. By their very nature they make no claim to objectivity, hence the importance of studying them within a context provided by the historian. In this connection it is worth making the general point that, under the 'Thirty Year Rule', the government documents for the 1930s and '40s have now become available to the researcher. This (together with the release of many collections of private papers) has led to a great deal of re-thinking and rewriting on the period in the last ten years or so, particularly on the contentious issue of Appeasement (see Kennedy's article cited below). Students should at least be aware of some of the more important new ideas on the period engendered by this significant historical research.

Visual evidence is also important and abundant for this period. The films made by the British Universities Film Council (based on contemporary films, newsreels etc.) on 'The Munich Crisis', 'Neville Chamberlain', and 'Stanley Baldwin', are outstanding. Contemporary political cartoons are similarly important. Those by David Low, showing a leftish point of view and published in the *Evening Standard*, are the most famous and brilliant. His published collections, such as, *Years of Wrath: A Cartoon History 1932–1945*, Gollancz, 1949, are now difficult to get hold of, but a few are reproduced below. 'Oral history,' though generally used more by the social historian, can be illuminating. A good example is Francis Williams's interviews with Attlee in *A Prime Minister Remembers*, Heinemann, 1961.

Political biographies vary enormously in quality and length, and very few can be strongly recommended to the student. On Churchill, the following can: Martin Gilbert (ed.) *Churchill*, Great Lives Observed, Prentice-Hall, 1967; A. J. P. Taylor *et al.*, *Churchill: Four Faces and the Man*, Allen Lane, 1969; Henry Pelling, *Winston Churchill*, Macmillan, 1967; R. R. James, *Churchill: A Study in Failure*, Penguin edn, 1981; Piers Brendan, *Churchill: A Brief Life*, Secker and Warburg, 1984. A major political biography is David Marquand, *Ramsay Macdonald*, Cape, 1977 – this is rather long, but sections of it (on the crisis 1931, for example) are outstanding and can be used separately. There is now an admirable biography of *Attlee* by Kenneth Harris, Weidenfeld and Nicolson, 1982. There are good short essays in J. P. Mackintosh (ed.) *British Prime Ministers in the Twentieth Century*, 2 vols, Weidenfeld, 1978.

On the general political history of the period, the most stimulating book is A. J. P. Taylor, *English History 1914–45*, OUP, 1965. A wider and outstanding survey is Martin Pugh, *The Making of Modern British Politics 1867–1939*, Blackwell, 1982. John Stevenson and Chris Cook, *The Slump*, Quartet Books edn, 1979, is essential for the politics of the 1930s. Post-war political history is covered briefly and lucidly in Alan Sked and Chris Cook, *Post-War Britain*, Penguin, 1979.

There are a number of useful books for the student about the political parties themselves. On the Conservative Party there is an essay by David Dilks, 'Baldwin and Chamberlain', and one by John Ramsden, 'From Churchill to Heath' in Lord Butler (ed.) *The Conservatives*, Allen and Unwin, 1977. For a longer historical perspective there is Robert Blake, *The Conservative Party from Peel to Churchill*, Eyre and Spottiswoode 1970, new edn, Fontana 1985. On the Labour Party are the following: Paul Adelman, *The Rise of the Labour Party 1880–1945*, Longman 1972, 2nd edn 1986;

Robert Skidelsky, *Politicians and the Slump*, Penguin edn, 1970; Chris Cook and Ian Taylor (eds.) *The Labour Party*, Longman, 1980 – a group of analytical essays; Roger Eatwell, *The 1945–51 Labour Governments*, Batsford, 1979; and (for reference) the recent detailed study by Kenneth O. Morgan, *Labour in Power 1945–51*, OUP, 1984. Also Michael Sissons and Philip French, *Age of Austerity 1945–51*, Penguin edn, 1964 contains a group of appealing essays on such topics as, 'Sir Stafford Cripps', 'Partition in India' and 'Bevan's Fight with the BMA'. The minor parties are covered adequately in Chris Cook, *Short History of the Liberal Party*, Macmillan, 1976; Henry Pelling, *The British Communist Party*, Black, 2nd edn, 1975; Colin Cross, *The Fascists in Britain*, Barrie and Rockliff, 1961.

On topics such as foreign policy the standard general survey is W. N. Medlicott, *British Foreign Policy since Versailles*, Methuen, 2nd edn, 1968. For the debate on Appeasement, the best short surveys are now D. C. Watt, 'The Historiography of Appeasement', in A. Sked and C. Cook (eds.) *Crisis and Controversy: Essays in honour of A. J. P. Taylor*, Macmillan, 1976, and Paul Kennedy, 'Appeasement', *Reading History, History Today*, October 1982. Good analyses include William R. Rock, *British Appeasement in the 1930s*, Arnold, 1977; Christopher Thorne, *The Approach of War 1938–9*, Macmillan, 1967; Anthony P. Adamthwaite, *The Making of the Second World War*, Allen and Unwin, 1977 – text and documents. Special aspects are discussed in Michael Howard, *The Continental Commitment*, Temple Smith, 1971 – the links between British foreign policy and defence; Neville Thompson, *The Anti-Appeasers*, OUP, 1971; and J. F. Naylor, *Labour's International Policy*, Weidenfeld, 1969. Two different points of view on Appeasement by one historian, Michael Gilbert, are displayed in Michael Gilbert and Richard Gott, *The Appeasers*, Weidenfeld, 1963; and Michael Gilbert, *The Roots of Appeasement*, Weidenfeld, 1966.

On the Second World War the outstanding book on the political side of the war is Paul Addison's fascinating study, *The Road to 1945*, Quartet Books edn, 1977. Two very good studies are Henry Pelling, *Britain and the Second World War*, Fontana, 1970; and Angus Calder, *The People's War*, Panther edn, 1971.

On the general election of 1945 are William Harrington and Peter Young, *The 1945 Revolution*, Davis Poynter, 1978, and Henry Pelling, 'The 1945 General Election Reconsidered', in *Historical Journal*, vol. 23, 1980.

# 1 Ramsay MacDonald and the crisis of Labour 1929–31

Since 1931, when Ramsay MacDonald became head of a National government dominated by Conservatives and Liberals, he has been regarded as a 'traitor' to the Labour Party – a standing reproach to all future Labour leaders who might be tempted in peace-time into pacts or alliances with the party's enemies. Yet Emanuel Shinwell (who served as MacDonald's colleague in the second Labour government (1929–31)) writes the following:

## 1.1

To dismiss MacDonald as a traitor is nonsense. His contribution in the early years was of incalculable value. His qualities as a protagonist of Socialism were of a rare standard. There has probably never been an orator with such natural magnetism combined with impeccable technique in speaking in the party's history. Before the First World    5
War his reputation in international Labour circles brooked no comparison . . .

Among his people in Scotland he could exert almost mesmeric influence . . . No one has ever completely explained the magnetism of MacDonald as a young man. He was the most handsome man I have    10
ever known, and his face and bearing can best be described as 'princely' . . . the people who loved him in those early days recognised it as an inborn quality. It also put him in Parliament . . . Leicester was intrigued about this Labour candidate who was the sole opponent of the Tory in 1906 . . . The immense Liberal vote was his    15
from the start . . . He won that election by emotionalism rather than intellect – as others before and since have won elections.

**Emanuel Shinwell, *Conflict without Malice*, Odhams, 1955, p. 113**

In 1918 MacDonald lost his parliamentary seat as a result of his anti-war stance. By the 1920s, however, he was the hero of the industrial working classes.

Ramsay, Ramsay, shout it
Don't be shy about it
Labour's day is sure to come –
We cannot do without it

chanted the children in the streets of Aberavon in South Wales when MacDonald was returned triumphantly to the House of Commons for that constituency in the general election of 1922. Shortly afterwards he was elected leader of the Parliamentary Labour Party. Two years later, in January 1924, amid scenes of enormous Labour enthusiasm, MacDonald became leader of a minority Labour government, dependent for its existence on the grudging and unwelcome support of the Liberals in the House of Commons.

The government lasted barely ten months: it cannot be said that its record, particularly on the domestic front, was an impressive one. Nevertheless, whatever weaknesses the government of 1924 revealed in policies and leadership, the reputation of MacDonald (and even of his ultra-orthodox Chancellor of the Exchequer, Philip Snowden) remained intact among the party rank-and-file. Indeed, MacDonald's position as Labour leader was if anything strengthened in the course of the next few years. For the abysmal failure of the General Strike in May 1926 seemed to indicate to the Labour movement at large the futility of relying on large-scale industrial action against a resolute Conservative government to secure its aims. A swing back to political action seemed indicated, and this was bound to benefit MacDonald – the personification of moderate, constitutional parliamentarianism.

Yet there was also growing disenchantment at this time on the Left of the Parliamentary Party with MacDonald's leadership and the whole philosophy of 'reformism'. Even Beatrice Webb, the Fabian Socialist (whose husband, Sidney, had served in the first Labour government) wrote this of the Labour leader in her diary in 1926:

**1.2**

The leader of the Labour Party was in his best form. He is an
attractive creature; he has a certain beauty in colouring, figure and
face, a delightful voice and an easy unpretentious manner . . . But his
conversation is not entertaining or stimulating – it consists of pleasant
anecdotes about political and society personages – occasionally some      5
episode in his own career – told with calculated discretion . . . Does
he ever exchange ideas? Certainly not with us . . . My general
impression is that J.R.M. feels himself to be *the* indispensable leader

of a new political party which is bound to come into office within his
life-time – a correct forecast, I think. He is no longer *intent* on social     10
reform – any indignation he ever had at the present distribution of
wealth he has lost: his real and intimate life is associating with the
beauty and dignity which wealth can buy and social experience can
direct. Ramsay MacDonald is not distinguished either in intellect or
character, and he has some very mean traits in his character. But he     15
has great gifts as a political leader, he has personal charm, he has
vitality, he is assiduous, self controlled and skilful . . . He has the
ideal appearance . . . but he is shoddy in character and intellect.

**The Diary of Beatrice Webb**, 1924–1932, ed. Margaret Cole,
Longman, 1956, pp. 11–12

## Questions

1     Analyse the views of MacDonald's character in documents 1.1 and
1.2. What do they show about attitudes within the Labour
movement towards MacDonald?
2     How do these documents help us to understand more clearly
MacDonald's role in the crisis of 1931?
3     Why are Shinwell and Webb important witnesses for an
understanding of MacDonald?
4     Why, nevertheless, should each of these documents be treated with
some caution as historical evidence?

Three years later, after the general election of 1929, MacDonald became
leader of a minority Labour administration for the second time, though on
this occasion, Labour did at least form the largest party in the House of
Commons. The major problem which faced the government – and one
which it had conspicuously failed to get to grips with in 1924 – was
unemployment. The number of unemployed was now already over a
million. Within a year the figure had doubled, and this in turn led to
mounting government expenditure on unemployment benefits. On taking
office the Prime Minister had appointed a small committee of ministers to
tackle the unemployment problem, including Sir Oswald Mosley. Young,
dynamic and ambitious, Mosley soon became disillusioned with the
dilatoriness of his colleagues and their failure to evolve any imaginative
plans for tackling unemployment. In January 1930 he produced his
famous *Memorandum* which suggested a long-term programme of economic reconstruction. To deal with unemployment in the short-run, he
proposed a government-financed plan of public works (especially road

construction), on which some two hundred million pounds was to be spent
over three years. Mosley describes what happened:

**1.3**

I became one of four Ministers charged with the unemployment
problem, with a room in the Treasury . . . J. H. Thomas was the
Minister primarily responsible and he also had a room in the same
building. The other two Ministers, Lansbury and Johnston, were
housed elsewhere, as they were responsible for the Office of Works    5
and the Scottish Office.

We were charged with the task of assisting a man who was entirely
incapable of understanding the subject, J. H. Thomas. It was
impossible to dislike Jimmy, as he required all the world to call him,
for he had many endearing qualities . . . However, in the 1929    10
Government the truth was soon obvious; Thomas found himself in a
sea of new problems completely out of his depth . . . Eventually I
saw no more of Thomas than was necessary, and got on with the job
of working out, within the departments, what seemed to me the real
policy necessary to deal with unemployment . . . I summarised my    15
series of proposals for dealing with unemployment in a document
which became known as the Mosley Memorandum. It was circulated
to Thomas and the Cabinet. If I recollect rightly, I notified him in
proper form that I intended to do this, but he complained that I
should first have discussed it with him.    20

It is part of the fatality of Labour that the leader is always
dependent on a balance of forces which inhibit action. The prisoner
leader is an invariable result of the whole structure, psychology and
character of the party. MacDonald simply could not afford to
dispense either with Thomas or Morrison, who chiefly obstructed    25
action – Thomas because he understood nothing and Morrison
because he was a narrow, rigid, vain little bureaucrat, devoid of vision
and incapable of movement beyond his office stool. As Minister of
Transport he rejected the schemes for national roads which thirty
years later had to be put through in a hurry . . . Thomas always    30
played safe. So did MacDonald, with the inevitable result not only of
my resignation but of the ultimate doom of his government. For my
part I felt quite simply that if I lent myself any longer to this cynical
harlequinade I should be betraying completely the people to whom
we had given such solemn pledges to deal with the unemployment    35

problem. I resigned in May 1930, and explained my proposals to deal
with unemployment in the House of Commons on May 28.

Before making my speech in the House of Commons on May 28, I
put the issue to the party . . . It is said that I made an error of
judgement in forcing the issue to the vote. On the contrary, I had          40
decided after deep reflection, coldly and deliberately in advance of
the meeting, to bring the party to a decision or eventually to leave. I
was not prepared to abandon millions of fellow-countrymen to
unemployment and near starvation . . . That is why I rejected the
appeal of Henderson and others not to take the issue to the vote at          45
the party meeting. Their argument was that the party was with me
but was not prepared to act; I must play for time. Only twenty-nine
voted with me. It remained my duty to try everything possible within
the Labour Party before making any other move, to give the rank and
file as well as the Parliamentary Party a chance to take action. This          50
meant going to the Party Conference in October 1930.

When the vote was taken at the Conference on the unemployment
issue, it was reckoned that the constituency parties voted ten to one
in my favour. Yet a single man with the power of Mr Bevin, who had
the Transport Workers' vote in his pocket, could out-vote the lot of          55
them; and he did . . . Even so, the result was a fairly close thing:
1,046,000 votes for us and 1,251,000 votes against.

**Sir Oswald Mosley,** *My Life,* **Nelson, 1968, pp. 230–7, 260–1**

George Strauss, then parliamentary secretary to the Ministry of Transport,
describes the meeting of the Parliamentary Labour Party to discuss
Mosley's vote of censure on the government's unemployment policy:

## 1.4

Mosley made an extremely eloquent speech which effectively played
on the dissatisfaction held by many members of the Party about the
Government's policy, and, certainly, won the sympathy of many
more. He pitched his speech on a very high note of emotion, and
managed to sustain a dramatic fervour throughout his appeal. It was          5
a magnificent piece of rhetoric which I wouldn't have missed for
worlds. Mosley's constructive suggestions appear to be weak, remote
and unconvincing. His figures were obviously fantastic. But most
members of the Party present felt that . . . as something had to be

done to stem the rising tide of unemployment, his plan should, at      10
least, be carefully considered, and in view of the apparent failure of
the Government to cope with the matter, they certainly – that is, the
Government – deserved some censure. The platform was plainly
nervous as to the outcome of the meeting after Mosley's fine speech.
MacDonald spoke next, but his vague phrases carried no conviction      15
... J. H. Thomas made a few words in his most lachrymose and
emotional vein. 'It was', he said, 'the most humiliating day of his life'
... The tenor of the discussion was this: that, while all agreed that
more should and could be done to cope with the unemployment
problem ... it was highly undesirable from the Party point of view,    20
that the censure motion that Mosley had moved should be put to a
vote. This point was put by Henderson in winding up the debate ...
Mosley insisted on putting it to the vote. Instantly, all the support
and sympathy he had received deserted him. A vote was taken ...
which showed that he had only 29 votes in his favour and 210 against   25
him. Mosley's action in refusing to withdraw ... was a grave
misjudgement of the feeling of the meeting and a tactical blunder.
Had he agreed to do so, Mosley's position in the party would have
been exceedingly strong. Now, as it is, he's looked upon with
complete lack of confidence by the Labour group as a whole.            30

**George Strauss, from Robert Skidelsky, *Politicians and the Slump*,
Macmillan, 1967, pp. 210–11**

**1.5**

**Cartoon by David Low, *Evening Standard*, 1930**

## Questions

1     What does Mosley mean by 'a balance of forces' within the Labour
      Party which inhibits action by the leader [**1.3, line 22**]? Has this
      always been true of Labour governments?
2     One historian refers to Mosley's 'bold and imaginative plans for an
      expansionist economic policy'; Strauss calls them 'weak, remote and
      unconvincing' [**1.4, line 7**]. How do you account for these differing
      points of view?
3     What point is document **1.5** making about MacDonald's handling of
      the issues? How fair do you think this is?
4     What evidence do you find in documents **1.3** and **1.4** to support this
      point of view?
5     What do documents **1.3** and **1.4** reveal about the qualities and
      defects of Mosley as a politician at this time?

In the summer of 1931 the Treasury was faced with a deepening financial
crisis as a result of bank failures in Central Europe and diminishing gold
reserves in Britain. It was at this point, on 31 July, that the Report of the all-
party May Committee, which had been set up by the Prime Minister in the
spring to report on the nation's finances, was published:

**1.6**

## THE ECONOMY REPORT

The majority report of the Economy Committee answers in drastic
and challenging fashion the question how the national finances can be
made to balance. The Report estimates that next year . . . the gap
between revenue and expenditure will be no less than £120,000,000.      5
It suggests economies totalling £96,500,000, and hints that the gap
might be further closed if some plan could be devised for imposing
further sacrifices on all incomes whether derived from public sources
or not. In the list of possible economies no branch of public
expenditure has escaped a thorough review . . . but the conclusions of   10
this review differ widely as between the different items. Broadly
speaking, the salaries of the Civil Service and the scale of the Defence
Forces escape censure; but of the total economy of £96,500,000
suggested the Report proposes that no less than £66,500,000 shall be
saved upon the cost of unemployment insurance, nearly £14,000,000    15
upon the cost of education, and nearly £8,000,000 upon the schemes

financed out of the Road Fund. Apart from a number of proposals, including a drastic cut in housing subsidies . . . it is clear that over the whole of the rest of public expenditure the Report has been able to find possible economies totalling only some £8,000,000. The broad     20 conclusion therefore is a repetition of the old lesson that economy depends on policy, and an assertion that present policy conforms to reasonable standards of economy except in relation to what are known as the Social Services.

*The Times*, 1 August 1931

All the members of the government accepted in principle the view of the Treasury and the Bank of England that confidence in the pound must be restored through a balanced budget, and that this could only be achieved by cutting government expenditure. How exactly this was to be realised was the task of the Cabinet Economy Committee of five members (MacDonald, Snowden, Henderson, Thomas and Graham) which got to work on 12 August.

After considerable discussion the Cabinet Economy Committee eventually agreed on cuts of 78 million pounds, including a ten per cent cut in unemployment benefit of 43.5 million pounds. But they refused to consider any reduction in the *standard rate* of benefit, and this soon became the nub of the whole dispute both within and outside the Cabinet during the next twelve days of crisis. The Cabinet, which met on 19 August, criticised the May Committee's and Cabinet Economy Committee's proposals and agreed provisionally on cuts of only 56 million pounds, including reductions in unemployment benefit of about 22 million pounds. The Prime Minister, who had already been in touch with the leaders of the Opposition, met a delegation from the TUC on the following evening to hear their suggestions. He describes the meeting in his diary:

**1.7**

[The delegation] included Citrine, Bevin . . . Their statement was that they were not to support the policy indicated by us in the afternoon, that we could balance the Budget by taxing the rentier, suspending the Sinking Fund and such like, but no economies. Chancellor replied and I observed that all I had to say was that their     5 observations did not touch our problem arising out of immediate financial necessity. They withdrew. It was practically a declaration of war. I was very tired and snatched a few minutes rest whilst Henderson once more told us what he had proposed days ago and

how everything had been initiated by him – except the things
opposed by the T.U.C. people. He surrendered. He proposed to
balance the Budget with insignificant economies, keep the
Unemployed assistance what it is now . . . suspending Sinking Funds
(which he stated many times was his proposal) made days ago . . .
and putting on a revenue tariff. How tired of it all one feels. We had
a rather pointless discussion without concentrating on the one point
of any importance: 'Are we to go on?'. Henderson never showed his
vanity and ignorance more painfully. I told them to go to bed and we
rose at 11 p.m. I was depressed and saw nothing but great
humiliation for us all. The T.U.C. undoubtedly voice the feeling of
the mass of workers. They do not know and their minds are rigid and
think of superficial appearances and so grasping at the shadow lose
the bone.

**David Marquand, *Ramsay MacDonald*, Cape, 1977, pp. 620–1**

## Questions

1     With reference to document **1.6**,
    (i) Why did the May Committee recommend such drastic cuts in
       unemployment benefit?
   (ii) What did the Committee hope to achieve through its overall
       programme of cuts?
 (iii) Why did MacDonald and Snowden accept the Committee's
       aims so easily?
 (iv) Why did the publication of the Committee's Report worsen
       rather than improve the immediate financial position?

2     Why did MacDonald feel it necessary to consult
    (i) the Opposition leaders, and
   (ii) the leaders of the TUC, about the government's discussions on
       cuts?

3     'It was practically a declaration of war' [**1.7**]. Is this a reasonably
    accurate view of the relations between the Prime Minister and the
    TUC during the rest of the August crisis?

The Cabinet met again on Friday 21 August, when a majority of members
insisted on sticking to the figure of 56 million pounds in cuts already
agreed upon, even though this had been rejected by the opposition leaders
as quite inadequate. The financial crisis now took a turn for the worse
when that very evening the Bank of England insisted that immediate
credits were needed from New York and Paris to staunch the accelerating

drain of gold, and that they were only likely to be forthcoming if the government accepted a further 20 million pounds in cuts, including – as a symbol of its resolution – a ten per cent cut in the standard rate of unemployment benefit. The Labour Cabinet, however, remained unprepared to make any major concession. The government now approached its 'moment of truth'. At its meeting on Sunday evening, 23 August, only one item was discussed: should the ten per cent cut be accepted?

## 1.8

Conclusions of a Meeting of the Cabinet held at 10 Downing Street, SW1, on Sunday 23rd August 1931 at 7 p.m.

The Prime Minister informed the Cabinet that a situation had now to be faced of a peculiarly difficult character because, if the Labour Party was not prepared to join with the Conservative and Liberal 5 Parties in accepting the proposals as a whole, the condition mentioned in Mr. Harrison's message regarding a national agreement would not be fulfilled.

So far as he was concerned, he was strongly in favour of such acceptance while at the same time making it clear that the scheme 10 represented the extreme limit to which he was prepared to go.

The Country was suffering from lack of confidence abroad. There was, as yet, no panic at home but the Prime Minister warned the Cabinet of the calamitous nature of the consequences which would immediately and inevitably follow from a financial panic and a flight 15 from the pound. No one could be blind to the very great political difficulties in which the giving effect to the proposals as a whole would involve the Government.

But when the immediate crisis was over and before Parliament met, it would be possible to give the Labour Party that full 20 explanation of the circumstances which had rendered it necessary for the Government to formulate such a drastic scheme, which could not be given at the moment. The only alternative was a reduction of not 10 per cent, but of at least 20 per cent, and he could not believe that the Labour Party would reject the proposals when they knew the true 25 facts of the position: he was confident, indeed, that a majority of the Party would accept them. A scheme which inflicted reductions and burdens in almost every other direction, but made no appreciable cut

in Unemployment Insurance benefit, would alienate much support
and lose the Party their moral prestige which was one of their                    30
greatest assets. In conclusion, the Prime Minister said that it must be
admitted that the proposals as a whole represented the negation of
everything that the Labour Party stood for, and yet he was absolutely
satisfied that it was in the national interest to implement them if the
country was to be secured. He then pointed out that, if on this                    35
question there were any important resignations, the Government as a
whole must resign.

Each member of the Cabinet then expressed his views on the
question of the inclusion, or otherwise, in the proposals of the 10 per
cent reduction in Unemployment Insurance benefit. In the course of      40
these expressions of view, indications were given that, while a
majority of the Cabinet favoured the inclusion in the economy
proposals of the 10 per cent reduction in Unemployment Insurance
benefit, the adoption of this as part and parcel of the scheme would
involve the resignation of certain Ministers from the Government.                  45

Cabinet Minutes 46 (31)

## Questions

1    What were the 'proposals as a whole' [1.8, line 6]? Why did they
     represent 'the negation of everything that the Labour Party stood
     for' [line 32–33]?
2    Why was the support of the Conservative and Liberal leaders for the
     proposed ten per cent cut so significant?
3    What were the main reasons why MacDonald and his supporters
     approved of the ten per cent cut?
4    Why did Henderson and his supporters oppose the proposed cut?
5    Does subsequent history illuminate or justify the attitude of either
     group?

With the collapse of the Labour government that evening, most of its
members naturally expected that it would be replaced by a Conservative or
Conservative/Liberal administration. But earlier that morning (without
the knowledge of his colleagues) the Prime Minister had seen King George V,
when the idea of a National government containing or led by MacDonald
had already been mooted. On the following Monday morning MacDonald
again saw the King, together with the Opposition leaders, Samuel and
Baldwin, and they agreed to sink their differences and form a National
government. At noon MacDonald met his Labour Cabinet for the last time,

and announced to its bemused members that he had agreed to head a National government and asked for their support. Only three members agreed to follow him. At 2.30 p.m. he saw the junior ministers. That evening MacDonald noted in his diary:

**1.9**

> The culminating day – 10 [a.m.]: King, Bal, Sam: Decided only Nat Govt. wd do to meet the crisis and on urgent request of all, I consented to continue as PM . . . 12, Cabinet: Consternation when I reported but in meanwhile news of terrible run on Bank. It was plain that I should be left almost alone with Snowden, Thomas, Sankey.    5
> 'Finis' is being written. They chose the easy path of irresponsibility and leave the burdens to others. Henderson I knew, but as regards some others, I have once more experienced weak human nature. 2.30: Minor Ministers etc. Of course they were not to take the hard side. Their superiors had decided otherwise and whoever reduced unemp.    10
> pay whatever the necessity was doomed. The good fellows just bowed to what would be a popular cry; the intellectuals talked of their theories of banking and currency. So they went. The Chancellor was getting pessimistic as the desertions went on and I tried to cheer him up, but indeed it was a dreary matter. Still, we were right. – 3pm:    15
> Samuel and Baldwin – 4.10, King and formally resigned and kissed hands on accepting to form a Govt. This is a lonely job.

**David Marquand *Ramsay MacDonald*, Cape, 1977, p. 643**

Four days after the formation of the National government, the Labour movement issued a Manifesto condemning what had happened:

**1.10**

### A JOINT MANIFESTO
Opposition to new Government

The following manifesto was yesterday approved and issued by the joint meeting of the Trades Union Congress General Council, the National Executive Committee of the Labour Party, and the    5
Consultative Committee of the Parliamentary Labour Party:

A financial crisis, the true causes of which have not been publicly explained, has brought about the sudden resignation of the Labour Government.

Forces in finance and politics made demands which no Labour          10
Government could accept. A new Coalition Government, for which
the Labour movement repudiates all responsibility, has been formed.
It is a Government of persons acting without authority from the
people.

It is determined to attack the standard of living of the workers in     15
order to meet a situation caused by a policy pursued by private
banking interests in the control of which the public has no part.

It seeks to enforce a complete change in national policy . . .
primarily because financial interests have decided that this country is
setting a bad example to other countries in taxing the rich to provide    20
for the necessities of the poor.

Fundamentally, it is an attempt to reverse the social policy which
in this country has within limits provided for the unemployed, the
aged, the sick etc . . . Unemployment benefit is attacked on the
ground that it strengthens resistance to wage cuts . . .                  25

The new government's policy has yet to be fully disclosed, but the
knowledge that it is irrevocably committed to serious cuts . . . has
roused the entire Labour movement to determined opposition.

The justification offered for these methods is the existence of a
financial crisis which has been aggravated beyond measure by            30
deliberately alarmist statements in sections of the Press and by a
protracted campaign that has created the impression abroad that
Great Britain is on the edge of bankruptcy. Nothing could be farther
from the truth . . .

If the will were present we could overcome the immediate           35
difficulty by mobilising the country's foreign investment, by a
temporary suspension of the Sinking Fund, by taxing . . . unearned
income . . . and by measures to reduce the burden of War debts. The
phrase 'equality of sacrifice' has been invoked as a justification for
cuts in social expenditure, but no comparable sacrifice has so far been    40
demanded from the wealthier sections of the community . . .

The present crisis is essentially part of a bigger one . . .

*The Times*, 28 August, 1931

## Questions

1     What can we learn from document **1.9** about MacDonald's reasons
      for agreeing to head a National government?

2     Why did the majority of the members of MacDonald's second
      Labour government refuse to join the National government?
3     How sound is the analysis in document **1.10** of the causes of the
      resignation of the second Labour government and the formation of
      the National government?
4     (i)  Why are the authors of the Labour Manifesto sceptical about
           the reality of the financial crisis?
      (ii) What practical measures do they propose to deal with the
           country's immediate financial problems?
5     'The new government's policy . . . has roused the entire Labour
      movement to determined opposition' **[1.10, line 28]**. To what extent
      was this true?
6     'The present crisis is essentially part of a bigger one' **[line 42]**. What
      point is being made here?
7     Do you see any parallels between the views expressed here in
      opposition to the National government, and those of the Labour
      movement since 1979 in opposition to the Thatcher government?

The formation of the National government and the introduction of the ten
per cent cut in the dole and other economies in Snowden's September
Budget did little to settle the financial crisis. Credits *were* obtained from
New York and Paris, but the drain on gold continued and Britain
abandoned the Gold Standard on 21 September 1931. MacDonald then
saw the need for a general election to restore national unity and
confidence, and in October he appealed for a 'doctor's mandate' to deal
with the nation's economic health. The result of the general election was
an overwhelming victory for the National government.

## 1.11

### A NATIONAL VICTORY

The General Election has given the National Government the
greatest majority ever recorded in British political history. Only some
half-dozen results are to come, and these are certain to be favourable
to the Government, whose majority in the House of Commons will         5
therefore be in the neighbourhood of 500. The victory of the Prime
Minister, against the full force of the Socialist Party machine and
against the heaviest pressure of the Trade Union organisation, stands
out among many magnificent achievements . . .

It is widely reported that this determination to vote National was          10
particularly remarkable among the women of all parties; but it is clear
also that appreciation of the vital issue – namely, whether the
purchasing power of housekeeping money was to endure or perish –
was by no means confined to women.

The power of the British people to grasp economic truths – and          15
their courage in facing unpalatable truths – is the first unquestionable
fact which emerges from this election. But it is equally beyond
question that this power would not have been revealed to so
magnificent an extent if the election had been fought on party lines.
The second and even more important conclusion, therefore, is that          20
this victory is a National victory and not a party victory, and that
conclusion is proved by every subsidiary circumstance . . . Moreover
the tremendous majorities obtained nearly everywhere by National
candidates – very frequently over 20,000 and ranging up to 51,000 at
Hendon and 62,000 at Brighton – cannot have been obtained merely          25
by the usual transfer of votes from one party to another. They were
in fact frequently obtained by Liberal and by Labour as well as by
Conservative supporters of the Government, and were not party
majorities in any sense of the word. A further proof lies in the
exceedingly high percentage of the electorate which went to the poll.          30
The figure is over seventy-nine per cent, and completely disproves
the hypothesis that there were any considerable abstentions for party
reasons.

The verdict of the electorate is therefore as deliberate as it is
decisive. These enormous majorities do not mean that people have          35
voted blindly anti-Labour or anti-free trade or anti-any of the minor
issues of politics. They mean, broadly speaking, that the nation has
passed judgement on leaders who have got into difficulties; who
admitted the difficulties and then (all but a courageous handful) ran
away from them; and who finally strove to escape judgement by          40
fighting the election on the crudest cries of class and party. They
have suffered for their own misjudgement of the intelligence and the
courage of the nation. But a condemnation so complete is, or should
be, in itself a sufficient lesson how to regard it. There should be no
crowing either in general or over individuals, but only sober          45
satisfaction that the calibre of the British democracy has been shown
so unmistakably superior to the low opinion formed of it by the
defeated.

*The Times*, 29 October 1931

## Questions

1      Explain the reference to 'the vital issue . . . whether the purchasing power of housekeeping money was to endure or perish' [**1.11, line 12–13**].

2      Why did the Labour Party do so badly in the 1931 election, according to *The Times?* Do you regard it as a reasonably objective view?

3      In what sense can the election be regarded as a personal triumph for MacDonald?

4      Do you agree with the comment that 'this victory is a National victory and not a party victory' [**line 21**]?

5      'Few governments have entered office with higher hopes and wider goodwill, few have fallen less lamented by friends as well as foes'. Discuss this view of the second Labour government (1929–31).

Beatrice Webb, in her diary, reflects on the 1931 election results from the point of view of the historical development of the Labour Party:

### 1.12

The Parliamentary Labour Party has been not defeated but annihilated . . . On the Front Opposition Bench there will be only one ex-Cabinet Minister – George Lansbury; only two ex-Ministers of rank – Stafford Cripps and Attlee; with one or two ex-Under Secretaries and Household Officers. This Parliament will last four or          5
five years; and the Labour Party will be out of office for at least ten years. The capitalists will remain, for this fourth decade of the twentieth century, in complete and unchallenged control of Great Britain . . . Meanwhile the Labour Movement may discover a philosophy, a policy and a code of personal conduct all of which we          10
lack today. The desertion of the three leaders was not the cause of our defeat; it was the final and most violent symptom of the disease from which the Party was suffering . . .

The Great War and the world upheaval brought the Labour Party on to the Front Opposition Bench and transformed it into a definitely          15
Socialist party. Two spells of office and the embraces of the old governing class converted the more prominent leaders into upholders of the existing order. Gradually becoming conscious of their leaders' lack of faith, the P.L.P. rapidly disintegrated. The dramatic desertion of the three leaders on the eve of the battle turned a certain defeat          20

into a rout. But it revealed a solid core of seven million stalwart
Labour supporters, mostly convinced Socialists. Whether new leaders
will spring up with sufficient faith, will-power and knowledge to
break through the tough and massive defences of British profit-
making capitalism with its press and its pulpits, its Royalties and          25
House of Lords, its elaborate financial entanglements of credit and
currency all designed to maintain intact ancient loyalties, and when
necessary, promote panics in favour of the *status quo*, I cannot
foresee. Have we the material in the British Labour Movement from
which can be evolved something of the nature of a religious order – a        30
congregation of the faithful who will also be skilful technicians in
social reconstruction? What undid the two Labour Governments was
not merely their lack of knowledge and the will to apply what
knowledge they had, but also their acceptance, as individuals, of the
way of life of men of property and men of rank . . . The Labour              35
Party leaders have shown that they have neither the faith, the code of
conduct, nor the knowledge needed for the equalitarian state

*The Diary of Beatrice Webb*, 1924–32, Longman, 1956, pp. 294–5

## Questions

1    What posts had been held in the second Labour government by
     Cripps, Attlee and Lansbury? Why was their electoral survival in
     1931 important for the history of the Labour Party in the 1930s?

2    In what ways did the First World War help to bring 'the Labour
     Party on to the Front Opposition Bench' and to transform it into 'a
     definitely Socialist party' [1.12, lines 15–16]?

3    'The desertion of the three leaders was not the cause of our defeat; it
     was the final and most violent symptom of the disease from which
     the Party was suffering' [lines 11–13]. What *was* the disease from
     which the Labour Party was suffering, according to Webb? Do you
     agree with her diagnosis?

4    Why, according to Webb, was it so difficult for Labour to 'break
     through the tough and massive defences of British profit-making
     capitalism' [line 24]? Give examples to prove or disprove her
     contention.

5    'But it revealed a solid core of seven million stalwart Labour
     supporters' [line 21]. What point is Webb making about Labour's
     electoral results?

6    What were the major practical problems that faced the Labour Party

in the aftermath of the 1931 electoral defeat? How far had these been overcome by the outbreak of the Second World War?

7   Referring to document **1.2**, how far were Webb's fears for the future of the Labour movement borne out by the events of 1929–31?

8   Was MacDonald's political position weakened or strengthened by the electoral results in 1931?

9   'He emerges from the record as a decent and likeable man, who, for most of his term of office, led his party with conspicuous skill'. Consider the justice of historian David Marquand's final verdict on MacDonald.

If the Labour Party was in a state of shock after the results of the 1931 general election, MacDonald's own political position was an extraordinarily difficult one. Though a tiny National Labour group existed in the House of Commons, in reality the Prime Minister was 'a man without a party', especially as the Conservatives now clearly dominated parliament. MacDonald's political isolation increased still further when the free trade ministers in the National government – Samuel, Reading and Snowden – resigned in 1932 after the policy of Protection was adopted. This coup served to emphasise how much the Prime Minister was now the prisoner of the Conservatives, even though on some issues – India and foreign policy especially – he was still able to exert his prime ministerial authority.

MacDonald's growing political weakness was worsened by age, ill-health and depression: by 1935 he was virtually 'the boneless wonder' of Churchill's cruel gibe. In June 1935, bowing to the inevitable, he gave way to Baldwin as Prime Minister, but unwisely carried on in the government as Lord President. His crumbling political prestige received a further heavy blow when he was defeated overwhelmingly by Emanuel Shinwell, at his old constituency of Seaham, in the general election of 1935. He crept back to the House of Commons in the following year as Independent MP for the Scottish Universities. But he was really a broken man. The end came in 1937. He resigned from the government that spring, and he died in November on board ship on a trip to Canada. His death hardly caused a ripple in the political world. As his biographer comments:

> Political careers often end cruelly. In recent British history, at least, few have ended more cruelly than MacDonald's.

**(David Marquand, *Ramsay MacDonald*, p. 700)**

# 2  Baldwin, Neville Chamberlain and the Conservative Party

The story of Stanley Baldwin's rise to power is quite unlike that of Ramsay MacDonald's. If the latter's election to the Labour leadership in 1922 was in some sense pre-ordained – given his outstanding abilities and record of service to the party – Baldwin's emergence as Conservative leader and Prime Minister was almost accidental. After years of obscure service as MP and junior minister, two events thrust Baldwin into the seat of power. The first was his outspoken attack on Lloyd George at the Carlton Club meeting of the Parliamentary Conservative Party in October 1922. This helped to precipitate the downfall of the Coalition government, and led to his own appointment as Chancellor of the Exchequer in the Bonar Law ministry that followed. The second factor was that, following Law's retirement through ill-health in May 1923, Baldwin's only real rival for the premiership was the Foreign Secretary, Lord Curzon, and as a peer he was considered an inappropriate choice in a period when Labour was the chief Opposition party in the House of Commons. The other senior Conservative leaders – Austen Chamberlain in particular – were Coalitionists, and had ruled themselves out of court by refusing to join Law's government in 1922. In this unexpected way Stanley Baldwin – 'a man of the utmost insignificance', according to Curzon – became Conservative leader and Prime Minister in 1923 at the age of fifty-six.

His tenure of office was a brief one. In a speech to the Conservative Party Conference at Plymouth in October 1923, Baldwin publicly declared, virtually out of the blue, his support for a Protectionist policy – fostering home produce and manufacture by import duties. Given Law's earlier pledge, Baldwin insisted on another general election to test public opinion. The result of the election of December 1923 was a clear verdict against Protection – a profound shock to the Conservative Party and a personal disappointment for Baldwin. As A. J. P. Taylor comments, 'For once he took the initiative, and learnt from his failure not to take it again'[1]. He shortly resigned, and at the beginning of 1924 MacDonald formed the first Labour government.

Stanley Baldwin was not a good Opposition leader: he lacked the debating skills and ruthlessness necessary for success in that role. Moreover, unlike many Conservatives, he had strongly supported Labour being given its chance to govern, and he had considerable sympathy with some aspects of the Labour creed. Like his hero, Disraeli, Baldwin hoped in opposition to 'educate his party' by improving its organisation and forcing it to adopt a more positive attitude to the rise of Labour. 'We are not going to fight the Labour Party by abuse,' he said in a speech in March 1924. 'It has to be fought in the only way that will ever win in this country, by substituting something better in the minds of the people'[2]. This was the theme that he hammered home to the Conservatives in a series of outstanding speeches inside and outside the House of Commons in 1924 – speeches which enabled him to impose his 'moral authority' on the party. This oratorical success was reinforced by the decisive Conservative victory in the general election of October 1924 which followed the collapse of the short-lived Labour government.

Harold Macmillan, who had just entered the House of Commons as MP for the industrial constituency of Stockton-on-Tees, describes the Prime Minister as he saw him during his second term of office:

**2.1**

On the Conservative side, Baldwin, the Prime Minister, was undoubtedly looked up to with something like affection by Members in every part of the House. The young and progressive wing of his party had a special regard for him. His speeches, particularly on industrial problems, struck just the right note which we thought              5
appropriate and illuminating . . . In these early days, I knew him as the man who had led us to a great electoral victory and who had made it possible, through his reputation for decency and fair-mindedness, to win the support of working men and women throughout the country . . .                                               10
He seemed to have inherited the true Disraelian tradition. The fact that he had played only a minor role in Lloyd George's great Coalition rather put people on his side. For the mood of the day – certainly at the beginning of the Parliament – was to be a little tired of the brilliant figures who had emerged during the war. If Bonar        15
Law had preached 'Tranquillity', Baldwin practised 'Peace in our Time'. He sat almost continuously in the House . . . He liked to watch and study his fellow Members. He often came into the smoking-room. It is true that he seldom spoke to anyone, but he would give one a friendly nod and we had a sense that he cared about       20
us, like the father of a young and growing family . . .
Baldwin's leadership of the Conservative Party was certainly firmly established in this Parliament . . . It was only as the Parliament proceeded that some of us began to feel some doubts . . . His intense and bitter dislike of Lloyd George struck us as exaggerated . . . He       25

affected to dislike 'intellectuals'. But that is a common pose of men of high intellectual qualifications; and Baldwin was certainly much more of a sensitive artist than of a rugged countryman . . .

Even to the most superficial observer it was clear that Baldwin operated at his best in a crisis, and this was followed by the need for       30
rest and recuperation. He was highly strung, nervous, and indeed the opposite in almost every way to the 'image' . . . which the party machine built up of him. It was said of Lord Liverpool that the secret of his policy was that he had none. To some extent this was true of Baldwin also . . . He was not a good administrator. He was an       35
influence, and an influence for good. The fact that he commanded the respect and even affection of the Labour Opposition confirmed our admiration for our leader . . . Nor should it be forgotten that . . . the Parliament of 1924–9 was a great constructive Parliament. It marked some of the greatest advances in social and administrative       40
reforms that have ever been made . . .

Harold Macmillan, *The Winds of Change 1914–39*, Macmillan, 1966, pp. 169–172

2.2

RAMSAY : " Call yerself a showman ; why, yer couldn't run a whelk stall."
STANLEY : " Well, and who wants to run a whelk stall ? "

**Cartoon by Strube, *Daily Express*, 17 May 1926**

2.3

Conservative Party, 1929

## Questions

1   Macmillan suggests that 'Baldwin operated at his best in a crisis' [2.1, line 30]. Give some examples to illustrate this point.

2   'Baldwin's leadership of the Conservative Party was certainly firmly established in this Parliament' [2.1, line 22]. Why was this so? Why was it not as true between 1929 and 1931?

3   What were the great 'advances in social and administrative reforms' [2.1, line 40] made by this government? Who were the ministers responsible for them? Would you agree that these policies marked the parliament of 1924 to 1929 as 'a great constructive Parliament'?

4   What building is represented in the Strube cartoon [2.2]? What is the cartoonist saying about Britain and the Conservative Party after the General Strike?

5   What particular Conservative policies are exemplified by the slogan 'Safety First!' in the poster [2.3]?

6   What does document 2.3 tell you about Baldwin's personal appeal to the voters?

7   Referring to documents 2.1, 2.2 and 2.3, what impression do you have of Stanley Baldwin? Which of these documents do you feel is most reliable as a piece of historical evidence?

As far as policy was concerned, the major achievements of Baldwin's second ministry were due to the work of individual ministers. The Prime Minister's main role, as he saw it, was to act as an 'honest broker' between his formidable ministerial colleagues, and set the tone of the government as a moderately reformist, humane and conciliatory administration. Nevertheless, Baldwin's Conservatism had its negative side. His policy of 'Safety First', particularly in industrial and economic matters, contributed to some extent to the Conservative failure at the general election of 1929, which led to the formation of the second Labour government.

Important sections of the party held Baldwin personally responsible for the defeat, and his henchman, J. C. C. Davidson, the party chairman was forced to resign in the following year. Nor was Baldwin any more effective now in Opposition than he had been during the first Labour government. This time, however, the opposition to Baldwin's leadership within the party was more widespread and more formidable. The Tory die-hards objected to his too favourable attitude to MacDonald's government (over Indian policy, for example), while the 'Press Lords', Rothermere and Beaverbrook, mounted a campaign in favour of Empire Free Trade (a euphemism for Protection) which blatantly and directly challenged Baldwin's control of the party. By the end of 1930 confidence in the leader appeared to be at an all-time low. Baldwin himself, tired and in low spirits, seemed all set to resign. By March 1931, however, he had recovered his nerve. In an electrifying speech on 18 March he trounced the arrogance of the 'Press Lords': 'What the proprietorship of these papers is aiming at is power, and power without responsibility – *the prerogative of the harlot throughout the ages*'[3]. The official Conservative candidate, Duff Cooper, was then returned against an Empire Crusader at the decisive St Georges by-election. In this way Baldwin's leadership was saved – permanently.

But though, as usual, Baldwin had won the war of words, the fundamental problems of policy still remained. In a way, therefore, the establishment of the National government a few months later was not unwelcome to the Conservative leader. He played little part in its formation, but he was happy to accept MacDonald, temporarily, as Prime Minister, and retire gratefully into the background as Lord President of the Council. There he could exercise his felicitous verbal and personal skills as a *national* statesman, while allowing Neville Chamberlain, the Chancellor of the Exchequer after the 1931 general election, to act as the real Conservative policy-maker in the government. As the latter admitted, 'I am bound to recognise that if I supply the policy and the drive, S.B. does also supply something that is perhaps even more valuable in retaining the floating vote'[4].

The government's commitment to Protection in 1932 removed the last major source of grievance between the rank-and-file and the Conservative leadership. In June 1935, therefore, bowing to the pressure of the Conservative majority in the House of Commons and aware of the growing feebleness and political isolation of MacDonald, Baldwin took over the office of Prime Minister. He consolidated his position by a decisive electoral victory a few months later. But he was now sixty-seven, and was faced with problems in foreign policy especially, which were complex, emotion-ally-charged and divisive.

In the earlier 1930s Britain's position abroad seemed threatened both by the expansionist policies of Japan in the Far East, and, after the advent of Hitler, by Germany's repudiation of the Treaty of Versailles and her commitment to rearmament. The National government's reaction to the changing international situation was slow and hesitant. In 1934, however, the Cabinet did come to two decisions. Firstly, it was agreed that the main threat to Britain came from Germany rather than Japan, mainly because of the vulnerability of these islands to air attack. As Baldwin said in a famous image, 'When you think of the defence of England you no longer think of the chalk cliffs of Dover; you think of the Rhine. That is where our frontier lies'. Secondly, Britain must rearm, and the main emphasis should be on the Air Force. But the commitment to rearmament was still half-hearted and the sums allotted were paltry even by the standards of the later thirties. This was partly because of economic difficulties. Even more important was Baldwin's profound belief that the British people were as yet too pacific in outlook to tolerate a dramatic rearmament programme.

The government also gave stronger support to the notion of 'collective security' through the League of Nations in order to maintain peace and deter aggression. A major diplomatic weapon against Germany during these years was an attempt, together with France, to maintain the friendship of Italy – a difficult endeavour owing to the increasingly aggressive postures of Mussolini. Italy's successful invasion of Abyssinia (Ethiopia) in the autumn of 1935 showed the fragility of Britain's hopes, and also helped to confirm the weakness of the League. The Hoare-Laval Pact (an attempt by Britain and France to buy off Mussolini, by offering territorial concessions to Italy) was followed by a public outcry and reduced even further the prestige of the government, and of Baldwin personally. 'Chips' Channon, a Conservative backbencher and man-about-town, describes the situation in the House of Commons:

**2.4**

19 December 1935

What a day. Sir Samuel Hoare has resigned . . . the House was packed. Sir Samuel Hoare sat in a corner of the 3rd bench, a place usually accorded to fallen Cabinet Ministers. He looked thin and ill . . .                                                                                        5

   There was considerable tension; many people, I amongst them, felt that the Government has behaved with almost incredible stupidity. It wobbled. First it displeased the Left-Wing by its seeming acceptance of the Hoare-Laval proposals, and then suddenly it made a volte-face, and dropped Hoare and the proposals, thus enraging the Right-Wing.    10
The Socialist Opposition have put down a Motion of Censure.

   At last Sam Hoare got up, and in a flash he had won the sympathy of the House by his lucidity, his concise narrative, his sincerity and patriotism. He told the whole story of his negotiations and added that not a country, save our own, has moved a soldier, a ship, an            15
aeroplane – was this collective action? He was a Cato defending himself; for 40 minutes he held the House breathless, and at last sat down, but not before he had wished his successor better luck, and burst into tears. I have never been so moved by a speech . . . to me it was the voice of a large section of sensible England: perhaps the        20
swan-song of a certain Conservative spirit . . . He was followed by

the Prime Minister, who was embarrassed and spoke lamely, though
he was honest enough to admit his mistake in accepting the proposals
. . . There were a few 'backbenchers' murmuring inaudible
complaints . . . If I had been in the House longer, I should have          25
struck a note of *reality*, and expressed the opinion of everyone one
meets – for God's sake, Mr Baldwin, make peace. Instead he has
allowed himself to be bullied by the Left-Wing Conservatives and the
Liberals . . . The vote was put and the Government won with a
majority of 232 . . . The Government is saved.                             30

23 December

Anthony Eden has been appointed Foreign Secretary by Mr Baldwin.
His appointment is a victory for 'The Left', for the pro-Leaguers. He
has had a meteoric rise, young Anthony . . . now at thirty-eight he is
Foreign Secretary. There is hardly a parallel in our history. I wish       35
him luck; I like him; but I have never had an exaggerated opinion of
his brilliance, though his appearance is magnificent.

**Chips: the Diaries of Sir Henry Channon**, ed. R. R. James, George
Weidenfeld and Nicolson, 1967, pp. 48–9

The corollary of Abyssinia was the acquiescence of France and Britain in
Germany's occupation of the Rhineland in 1936, while the outbreak of the
Spanish Civil War in the same year soon underlined the weaknesses of
their diplomacy in support of the farce of 'non-intervention'. On the other
hand, 1936 was the moment when Great Britain at last made a
determined commitment to rearmament: one and a half million pounds
were allotted, and the primary aim was to secure air parity with Germany
by 1939.

The years 1935–6 were not, therefore, happy ones for Baldwin. Even the
government's India Bill was opposed to the bitter end by a group of die-
hard Tories, spurred on by Winston Churchill. But the Prime Minister did
have one last triumph before he retired: his handling of the Abdication
Crisis in 1936. It is generally agreed that this was carried through with
consummate tact and skill. In May 1937 Baldwin resigned, accepted an
earldom, and was succeeded as Prime Minister by Neville Chamberlain.

## Questions

1      (i) What proposals were put forward by the League of Nations for
       obtaining an Italian withdrawal from Abyssinia? Why did they
       fail?

    (ii)  What were the terms of the Hoare-Laval Pact? Why was there
such an outcry in Britain against them?

    (iii)  What, according to Channon, were the differences between
'Left-wing' and 'Right-wing' Conservatives on the Abyssinian
crisis [2.4]? Is his use of these terms a helpful one when applied
to the Conservative Party at this time?

2    Was the Abdication Crisis an event of any importance in British
politics?

3    With particular reference to the documents quoted above, what
would you say were the merits and defects of Baldwin as
Conservative leader between 1923 and 1937?

Chamberlain's assumption of the premiership was virtually a foregone
conclusion. As Prime Minister, however, he cut a very different figure from
Baldwin. Harold Macmillan writes:

**2.5**

Next to Baldwin, the most effective force in the Government (1924–
29) was Neville Chamberlain . . . he was in a true sense Mayor of the
Palace. What he said in Cabinet or Council was in the end accepted.
So great was his activity that he did not hesitate to give help and
advice to his colleagues in other departments. Many of the plans    5
which were ultimately presented by other Ministers had their origin
in his tireless zeal.

    Chamberlain was not a favourite of the House, and he never
obtained that attention from the Opposition which it is necessary for
a leading Minister to secure. This was a defect partly of manner and    10
partly of feeling. He had a certain intellectual contempt for people
whose views he thought ridiculous; and most of the Labour Party he
put into that category. But he was not able to conceal this, and his
tone revealed a degree of sarcasm and even rudeness towards his
opponents, which is contrary to the true House of Commons    15
tradition, at least at the top . . . Nevertheless, he was a commanding
personality. His speeches were admirably prepared and argued. If his
voice was rasping and often weak, his Parliamentary style was good.
He marshalled facts and statistics with ease. His slim figure,
conventionally dressed (he usually wore a tail coat and stiff wing-    20
collar), his well-groomed appearance, his perfect self-control: all these
made him an outstanding Parliamentarian. I can still see him

standing at the box, erect and confident. But he was respected and feared rather than loved . . .

**Harold Macmillan,** *The Winds of Change 1914–39*, **Macmillan, 1966, pp. 313–14**

Though social and economic matters were not unimportant in Chamberlain's peace-time ministry, it was of course foreign affairs, and particularly the Prime Minister's pursuit of Appeasement, that dominated its activities. Chamberlain's policy of Appeasement had been described and defended by Sir Samuel Hoare, later Viscount Templewood, who was one of its leading exponents:

**2.6**

On the political side, appeasement, having been universally applauded, was still a term of faint praise rather than violent abuse. Since the time when Eden first used it with general approval during the debates on the German occupation of the Rhineland in 1936, it had been freely accepted into the reputable currency of political        5
discussion. It was a noble word, and at the time seemed to express a wise and humane policy. Appeasement did not mean surrender, nor was it a policy only to be used towards the dictators. To Chamberlain it meant the methodical removal of the principal causes of friction in the world. The policy seemed so reasonable that he could not believe        10
that even Hitler would repudiate it. Hitler at the time seemed genuinely anxious to live on good terms with the British Empire. He had obtained equality of status for his country, and needed a period of peace to consolidate his political power.

Chamberlain was not an autocrat who imposed his views on        15
doubting or hostile colleagues. Appeasement was not his personal policy. Not only was it supported by his colleagues; it expressed the general desire of the British people. This is a fundamental consideration in judging his action. Nothing is further from the truth than the myth that has been invented of his intolerant omnipotence.        20
Whilst the prime mover, he was never the dictator of the Government's policy . . . His colleagues supported him because they agreed with him, and in agreeing with him, they acted in accordance with the view of the great majority of his supporters in Parliament and a large body of public opinion in the country.        25

His personal influence was due to his mastery of facts, his clear
head and his inherited gift of incisive speech. As Prime Minister, he
took the closest interest not only in the Foreign Office, but in all the
Departments of State . . . In the Conservative Party, his qualities had
much the same influence as they had in Whitehall . . . The Party's        30
policy was constantly in his mind, and no Conservative Minister ever
took a more detailed interest in election programmes. It was not,
therefore, surprising that his position in the Party was unassailable.
    In the House of Commons, where it was no less secure, it was
further strengthened by his talent for debate. A party expects fighting   35
qualities in its leader. Chamberlain delighted his followers not only
with his gifts of clear statement and keen argument, but still more,
with the evident pleasure that he showed in routing his enemies.

**Viscount Templewood, *Nine Troubled Years*, Collins, 1954, pp. 373–6**

'From the first', wrote Chamberlain, 'I have been trying to improve
relations with the two storm centres, Berlin and Rome.' One arm of this
policy was the Halifax Mission to Germany in November 1937, but this led
nowhere. The Prime Minister was determined, therefore, to push ahead
rapidly with talks with Italy to resolve outstanding differences, even if this
meant negotiations conducted without consultation with his own Foreign
Secretary. This was an important reason for Eden's resignation in
February 1938. In March 1938 German troops marched into Austria,
virtually without any protest from Britain and France. The Anschluss
made it almost inevitable that Hitler's gaze would next be focused on
Czechoslovakia, where a separate German minority existed in the
Sudetenland, strongly sympathetic to Nazism. It was their grievances –
real or supposed – that were used by Hitler to justify his vicious, stage-
managed, verbal assaults on the Czech state in the summer of 1938. His
eventual demand for the cession of Sudetenland precipitated the September Crisis, and led to Chamberlain's three dramatic flights to interview
Hitler personally – at Berchtesgaden (15–16 September), Godesberg (23–4
September) and Munich (29–30 September). Harold Nicolson describes
the famous scene in the House of Commons that preceded the Munich
meeting:

**2.7**

Diary 28 September 1938

I walk down to the House at 2.15 p.m. passing through Trafalgar

Square and Whitehall . . . As we get near the House of Commons there is a large shuffling, shambling crowd and people putting fresh flowers at the base of the Cenotaph. The crowd is very silent and anxious. They stare at us with dumb, inquisitive eyes.

The Prime Minister entered . . . He was greeted with wild applause by his supporters, many of whom rose in their seats and waved their order-papers. The Opposition remained seated.

Mr Chamberlain rose slowly in his place and spread the manuscript of his speech upon the box in front of him. The House was hushed in silent expectancy. From the Peers' Gallery above the clock the calm face of Lord Baldwin peered down upon the arena in which he himself had so often battled. Mr Chamberlain began with a chronological statement of the events which had led up to the crisis. He spoke in calm and measured tones and the House listened to him in dead silence . . .

The chronological method which he adopted increased the dramatic tension . . . He went on to describe his negotiations with the Czechs and the French and to tell us how he had felt it necessary himself to visit Herr Hitler 'as a last resort'. When he said these words, 'as a last resort', he whipped off his pince-nez and looked up at the skylight with an expression of grim hope. He then described his visit to Berchtesgaden. 'It was', he said with a wry grin, 'my first flight', and he described the whole visit as 'this adventure'. He said that his conversation with Herr Hitler had convinced him that the Fuhrer was prepared on behalf of the Sudetan Germans, 'to risk a world war'. As he said these words a shudder of horror passed through the House of Commons.

'I came back', he added, 'to London the next day'. The House was tense with excitement. He then told us how the Anglo-French plan was described by Hitler at Godesberg as 'too dilatory'. 'Imagine', he said, 'the perplexity in which I found myself'. This remark aroused a murmur of sympathetic appreciation from all benches.

'Yesterday morning', began the Prime Minister, and we were all conscious that some revelation was approaching. He began to tell us of his final appeal to Herr Hitler and Signor Mussolini. I glanced at the clock. It was twelve minutes after four. The Prime Minister had been speaking for exactly an hour. I noticed that a sheet of Foreign Office paper was being rapidly passed along the Government bench. Sir John Simon interrupted the Prime Minister and there was a momentary hush. He adjusted his pince-nez and read the document

that had been handed to him. His whole face, his whole body seemed
to change. He raised his face so that the light from the ceiling fell full
upon it. All the lines of anxiety and weariness seemed suddenly to          45
have been smoothed out; he appeared ten years younger and
triumphant. 'Herr Hitler', he said, 'has just agreed to postpone his
mobilisation for twenty-four hours and to meet me in conference with
Signor Mussolini and Monsieur Daladier at Munich'.

   That, I think, was one of the most dramatic moments that I have          50
ever witnessed. For a second, the House was hushed in absolute
silence. And then the whole House burst into a roar of cheering,
since they knew that this might mean peace. That was the end of the
Prime Minister's speech, and when he sat down the whole House
rose as a man to pay a tribute to his achievement.                          55

***Harold Nicolson's Diaries and Letters 1930–9***, ed. Nigel Nicolson,
1966

**2.8**

STILL HOPE

***Punch***, 21 September 1938

## Questions

1    What explanation does document **2.5** give for Chamberlain's not being a favourite of the House? How does he contrast with Baldwin?
2    What evidence is there in documents **2.6–2.9** that the policy of Appeasement expresses 'the general desire of the British people' [**2.6**, line 18]?
3    Would *you* have favoured Appeasement or not in the 1930s? Why?
4    What can be learned about the attitudes of the British public to the Munich crisis from documents **2.7** and **2.8**? Why did it arouse such emotions in the British public?
5    Chamberlain's first two visits to Hitler in September 1938 'were a diplomatic blunder of the first magnitude'. Discuss.
6    Why did Chamberlain believe that the Munich agreement had secured 'peace in our time'? Why did the anti-Appeasers regard it as 'a total and unmitigated defeat'?

Not all Conservatives supported the Munich settlement. Duff Cooper resigned from the government – the only Cabinet Minister to do so. About twenty MPs abstained in the vote that followed the debate, and they became the nucleus of the Conservative anti-Appeasement group that developed at this time (for Churchill's anti-Appeasement speech, see **6.3**). Yet their influence on government policy was negligible. As *The Spectator* commented in December 1938, 'Looking back on the last three months one could not help being struck by the amazing solidarity of the Conservative Party'[5]. Conservative solidarity was not really dissipated even after the German entry into Prague and the destruction of the Czech state in March 1939. 'Chips' Channon records his feelings in his diary:

**2.9**

15 March [1939]

Hitler has entered Prague, apparently, and Czechoslovakia has ceased to exist. No balder, bolder departure from the written bond has ever been committed in history. The manner of it surpasses comprehension and his callous desertion of the Prime Minister is stupefying. I can never forgive him. It is a great day for the Socialists and the Edenites. The PM must be discouraged and horrified. He acceded to the demand of the Opposition for a debate and the business of the House was altered. Then he rose, and calmly, but I

am sure with a broken heart, made a frank statement of the facts as        10
he knew them . . . I thought he looked miserable. His whole policy of
appeasement is in ruins. Munich is a torn-up episode. Yet never has
he been proved more abundantly right for he gave us six months of
peace in which we re-armed, and he was right to try appeasement. I
was relieved at how little personal criticism there was of the Apostle        15
of Peace . . .

The country is stirred to its depths, and rage against Germany is
rising.

**Chips: The Diaries of Sir Henry Channon**, ed. R. R. James, George
Weidenfeld and Nicolson, 1967, pp. 185–6

The Prime Minister realised the implication of the German invasion of
Czechoslovakia. Hitler's attitude, he now told the Cabinet, 'made it
impossible to continue to negotiate on the old basis with the new regime'[6].
The Prague coup was followed by 'a diplomatic revolution'[7]. Negotiations
were begun to provide a British guarantee against German aggression
towards Poland – clearly the next state on Hitler's list – and other smaller
European countries. This was followed in the summer by the abortive
military discussions with the Soviet Union, and a definite Anglo-French
commitment to Poland. The signature of the Soviet–German Pact on 23
August made war in effect inevitable. Hitler invaded Poland on 1
September 1939, and France and Britain declared war on Germany two
days later. 'Everything that I have worked for', said the Prime Minister,
'has crashed into ruins.'

It cannot be said that Chamberlain proved an effective war leader. The
uneasiness which the Opposition and many Conservative members felt at
his tepid war leadership came to a head after the Norwegian debacle in the
spring of 1940. Chips Channon describes the end of the traumatic debate
on a 'no confidence' motion that took place in the House of Commons on 8
May 1940. It marked a turning-point in the British handling of the war.

**2.10**

Then I voted . . . I went back to the Chamber and took my seat
behind Neville. 'We're alright' I heard someone say, and so it seemed
as David Margesson came in and went to the right, the winning side
of the table, followed by the other tellers. '281 to 200' he read, and
the Speaker repeated the figures. There were shouts of 'Resign –        5
Resign' . . . and that old ape Josh Wedgewood began to wave his
arms about and sing 'Rule Britannia'. Harold Macmillan, next to

him, joined in, but they were howled down. Neville appeared bowled
over by the ominous figures, and was the first to rise. He looked
grave and thoughtful and sad; as he walked calmly to the door, his    10
supporters rose and cheered him lustily and he disappeared. No
crowds tonight to cheer him, as there were before and after Munich –
only a solitary little man, who had done his best for England.

*Chips: the Diaries of Sir Henry Channon*, ed. R. R. James, George
Weidenfeld and Nicolson, 1967, p. 247

## Questions

1    Why did Channon see Hitler's invasion of Czechoslovakia as a
'callous desertion of the Prime Minister' [2.9, line 5]? Is the rest of
the document a fair evaluation of Chamberlain's role after the
German annexation of Czechoslovakia?

2    What do the voting figures '281 to 200' [2.10] reveal about the
attitudes of the Parliamentary Conservative Party to the government
by 8 May 1940?

3    On the evidence presented in this chapter, would you agree that
Chamberlain 'had done his best for Britain'?

## References

1    A. J. P. Taylor, *English History 1914–1945*, Oxford University Press, 1965,
p. 207

2    Wickham Stead, *The Real Stanley Baldwin*, Nisbet, 1930, p. 71

3    R. R. James, *The British Revolution*, Methuen, 1978, p. 514

4    John Ramsden, *The Age of Balfour and Baldwin*, Longman, 1978, p. 331

5    Neville Thompson, *The Anti-Appeasers*, Oxford University Press, 1971, p. 199

6    W. R. Rock, *British Appeasement in the 1930s*, Arnold, 1977, p. 19

7    A. P. Adamthwaite, *The Making of the Second World War*, Allen and Unwin,
1977, p. 86

# 3  Opposition politics in the 1930s

The traumatic events of 1931 had a profound effect on the Labour Party, and to a large extent conditioned its behaviour in the 1930s and even beyond. The party was now faced with the task of finding new leaders, repairing its organisation and finances, restoring party unity and morale, and developing a convincing programme. It was only slowly that these problems were overcome. By 1935, however, the Labour Party was beginning to recover. It had made considerable gains in local government – the London County Council was captured in 1934 – and had won ten by-elections (though it is fair to point out that these were former seats recaptured, not electoral gains). This modest advance was perhaps a reflection of the lack of real unity within the party, particularly over questions of foreign policy. In November 1935 Baldwin called a general election. Below are the main points of the Labour Party's electoral Manifesto:

3.1

### LABOUR MANIFESTO 1935
(The Labour Party's Call to Power!)

Four years have passed since the 'National' Government obtained a swollen majority in the House of Commons on a campaign of fraud, misrepresentation and panic . . .                                                    5

### Four Barren Years

At the end of four years the country faces the grim spectacle of two million workless with an army of well over a million and a half people on the Poor Law, and with the deepening tragedy of the distressed areas. Whilst doles of varying kinds have been dispensed on a lavish     10
scale to industry after industry, not a single constructive step has been taken to improve the lot of the people.

The Government has robbed the unemployed of benefit and subjected them to a harsh and cruel household means test . . .

It has retarded the building of houses to let, curtailed schemes          15
of public works, and discouraged the development of the social
services . . .

## The International Situation

The Government has a terrible responsibility for the present
international situation. It did nothing to check the aggression of          20
Japan in the Far East, and thus seriously discredited the League of
Nations and undermined the Collective Peace System.

It has wrecked the Disarmament Conference by resisting all the
constructive proposals made by other States . . . The Government
has helped to restart the arms race, and it failed to make Mussolini       25
understand, that if he broke the peace in Africa, Britain would join
with other nations in upholding the authority of the League . . . This
Government is a danger to the peace of the world and to the security
of this country.

## Labour's Peace Policy          30

The Labour Party calls for a reversal of this suicidal foreign policy. It
seeks wholehearted co-operation with the League of Nations . . . It
stands firmly for the Collective Peace System.

Labour will efficiently maintain such defence forces as are
necessary and consistent with our membership of the League; the            35
best defence is not huge competitive national armaments, but the
organisation of collective security against any aggressor and the
agreed reduction of national armaments everywhere.

Labour will propose to other nations the complete abolition of all
national air forces . . . large reductions by international agreement in    40
naval and military forces . . . A Labour Government would also seek
full international co-operation in economic and industrial questions,
with a view to increasing trade and raising standards of living
throughout the world, and removing the economic causes of war . . .

## A Bold Policy of Socialist Reconstruction          45

At home, the Labour Party will pursue its policy of Socialist
Reconstruction. Labour has already put before the country, boldly
and clearly, schemes of public ownership for the efficient conduct, in

the national interest, of banking, coal . . . transport, electricity, iron
and steel, and cotton.                                                        50

   It has also declared for the public ownership of land . . . Labour is
pledged to a comprehensive programme of industrial legislation, so as
to secure reasonable hours and conditions of employment for all
workers . . . Labour in power would attack the problem of the
distressed areas by special steps designed to deal with the root causes    55
of their troubles, as part of a vigorous policy of national planning . . .

   Labour asks the Nation for a Parliamentary Majority to promote
Socialism at home and Peace abroad.

**F. W. S. Craig, *British General Election Manifestos 1918–66*,
Parliamentary Research Services, Chichester, 1970, pp. 81–3**

## Questions

1      (i)  How justified was Labour's attack in the Manifesto [3.1] on the
            National government's foreign policy?
      (ii)  To what extent did Labour provide a coherent and realistic
            alternative?
2      (i)  What did the Labour Party mean by 'Socialism' according to
            this Manifesto?
      (ii)  On what grounds might a spokesperson for the National
            government have attacked the final section of the Manifesto?

The influence of the Left in British politics was seen not only within the
Labour Party, but in groups and parties outside it. In 1932 the
Independent Labour Party had disaffiliated from the Labour Party on the
grounds that it still supported 'reformism'. Under the leadership of men like
Maxton and Brockway, it returned to its roots as a sectarian socialist party.
More important in the 1930s, as reactions to the Spanish Civil War
revealed, was the British Communist Party. This had been founded in
1920 in the aftermath of the enthusiasm aroused by the Russian
Revolution, largely as a working-class party. Marxist, militant, and tied
hand and foot to the Communist leadership in Moscow, it was alien to the
traditions of the Labour Party, which consistently refused to accept its
requests for affiliation. The British Communist Party had considerable
influence in industrial affairs in the 1920s, but politically made little
headway. It had about six thousand members at that time, but this figure
rose rapidly in the following decade, reaching a total of about eighteen
thousand members on the eve of the Second World War. This transform-
ation was primarily due to the 'entry of the intellectuals' – the influx into

the party of middle-class recruits, often from the public schools and Oxbridge. The poet, John Cornford, was perhaps the archetypal Communist intellectual of the period. After graduating from Cambridge in 1936 he joined the International Brigade and was killed in action in Spain a few months later. He describes below the influence of Communism in the universities in 1936:

**3.2**

The last few years have seen a considerable growth of Communist
influence in the universities . . . The swing to the Left has not come
primarily because students are interested in politics in the abstract. It
has come because the actual conditions of their lives, the actual
problems with which they are confronted, force them steadily though      5
hesitatingly to a revolutionary position . . . Finally there are the
direct political results of the crisis . . . Manchuria and Mussolini's
invasion of Abyssinia have provided a very convincing proof of the
Communist thesis that wars arise out of the economic necessity
forcing capitalist nations to imperial expansion . . . for those who are   10
prepared to face the complexities of the situation, to face up to the
dangers and difficulties in a realistic way, the revolutionary solution
seems more and more necessary and inevitable. The next war will
produce more Wilfred Owens and less Rupert Brookes. And here too,
the consistent and unwavering fight of the U.S.S.R. to preserve the      15
peace at almost any cost, its willingness to make any concession for
peace and its complete freedom from any aggressive aims, is
contrasting more and more sharply with the military antics of the
Fascist powers and the shiftiness and two-faced policies of
'democratic' Britain and France. It is becoming more and more          20
patently clear that Soviet Communism not only stands for peace but
is winning all along the line on the economic front, whereas Fascism
is heading for war and economic disaster. For a long time the cry still
went up that they are both alike because there is no freedom . . .
[but] the Soviet system is in certain respects the highest form of       25
democracy yet seen . . .
   Out of the break-up of the standards of an entire class before
changing conditions of life, a compact revolutionary core is being
formed – a small minority still, but the most organised and efficient
of the minorities. The changes that are going on now, often            30

imperceptibly, but none the less steadily, will perhaps later assume a
national importance that very few of the actors in the present small-
scale events realise. But when the next crisis·that will shake the whole
system explodes, whether it is war crisis, economic crisis, or political
crisis, the relatively quiet and petty developments of these pre-war,          35
pre-crisis years will emerge in their real significance.

**John Cornford – a Memoir, ed. Pat Sloan, Cape, 1938, pp. 159–69**

John Cornford wrote the following poem during the Spanish Civil War:

**3.3**

Now the same night falls over Germany
And the impartial beauty of the stars
Lights from the unfeeling sky
Oranienburg* and freedom's crooked scars.
We can do nothing to ease that pain                                          5
But prove the agony was not in vain.

England is silent under the same moon,
From the Clydeside to the gutted pits of Wales.
The innocent mask conceals that soon
Here, too, our freedom's swaying in the scales.                              10
O understand before too late
Freedom was never held without a fight.

Freedom is an easily spoken word
But facts are stubborn things. Here, too, in Spain
Our fight's not won till the workers of all the world                        15
Stand by our guard on Huesca's plain
Swear that our dead fought not in vain,
Raise the red flag triumphantly
For Communism and for liberty.

* A German concentration camp

**John Cornford, from 'Full Moon at Tierz: before the Storming of
Huesca', in Robin Skelton, *Poetry of the Thirties*, Penguin, 1964, pp.
138–9**

John Cornford, 1936. From Pat Sloan (ed.) *John Cornford. A Memoir*, Cape, 1938, frontispiece

## Questions

1   What point is being made by Cornford in his reference to Owen and Brooke [**3.2, line 14**]?

2   With reference to documents **3.2 and 3.3**,
   (i)   what made Englishmen like Cornford turn to Communism in 1936?
   (ii)  what can be said for and against their commitment at the time?
   (iii) name two other men who became Communists at Cambridge in the 1930s and indicate why they achieved notoriety.

3   What reasons can you find in documents **3.2** and **3.3** to account for the Spanish Republican cause arousing such intense fervour in left-wing circles in Britain?

If Communism developed in this country in the 1930s as the major extremist movement on the Left, Fascism emerged as its counterpart at the opposite end of the political spectrum. This was due largely to one man – Oswald Mosley. In many ways a typical member of the English upper class, Mosley had begun his political career after war service as a Conservative, but had seceded to Labour in 1924. He was given office in MacDonald's second Labour government in 1929, and in 1931 (see Chapter 1) he resigned when his radical programme for dealing with unemployment was rejected by the Cabinet and Party. He then broke with Labour and formed the 'New Party', supported by a motley collection of politicians and intellectuals. The New Party was decimated in the general election of 1931. In October 1932 – by which time most of his earlier associates had abandoned him – Mosley formed the British Union of Fascists (BUF), and set out the ideas of the new organisation in *The Greater Britain:*

### 3.4

In Great Britain during the past ten years there have never been less than a million unemployed, and at present unemployment approaches the three million figure . . . We have tragic proof that economic life has outgrown our political institutions. Britain has failed to recover from the War period; and this result, however complicated by special      5
causes, is largely due to a system of Government designed by, and for, the nineteenth century . . . I believe that, under the existing system, Government cannot be efficiently conducted.

Hence the need for a New Movement, not only in politics, but in the whole of our national life. The movement is Fascist, (i) because it      10
is based on a high conception of citizenship – ideals as lofty as those which inspired the reformers of a hundred years ago: (ii) because it recognises the necessity for an authoritative state, above party and sectional interests . . . We seek to organise the Modern Movement in this country by British methods in a form which is suitable to and      15
characteristic of Great Britain. We are essentially a national movement, and if our policy could be summarised in two words, they would be 'Britain First'.

Fascism is the greatest constructive and revolutionary creed in the world. It seeks to achieve its aim legally and constitutionally, by      20
methods of law and order; *but in objective it is revolutionary or it is nothing.* It challenges the existing order and advances the constructive alternative of the Corporate State. To many of us this creed

represents the thing which we have sought throughout our political
lives. *It combines the dynamic urge to change and progress with the*       25
*authority, the discipline and the order without which nothing great can be*
*achieved* . . . The essence of Fascism is the power of adaptation to
fresh facts. Above all, it is a realist creed. It has no use for immortal
principles in relation to the facts of bread-and-butter; and it despises
the windy rhetoric which ascribes importance to mere formulae. The       30
steel creed of an iron age, it cuts through the verbiage of illusion to
the achievement of a new reality . . . We have seen the political
parties of the old democracy collapse into futility through the sterility
of committee government and the cowardice and irresponsibility of
their leadership . . . the only effective instrument of revolutionary       35
change is absolute authority. We are organised, therefore, as a
disciplined army, not as a bewildered mob with every member
bellowing orders. Fascist leadership must lead, and its discipline must
be respected.

The main object of a modern and Fascist movement is to establish       40
the Corporate State . . . Its achievement is revolution, but not
destruction. Its aim is to accept and use the useful elements within
the State, and so to weave them into the intricate mechanism of the
Corporate system.

**Oswald Mosley,** *The Greater Britain,* **BUF, 1932, pp. 11–16, 24–6,
150–1**

Within a year, Mosley had founded a party newspaper, *Blackshirt,* and
organised the BUF as a national, military-type political party. Its
propaganda effort was concentrated on marches and large-scale public
meetings, often accompanied by ugly scenes of violence. The two most
notorious incidents of this type were the Olympia Meeting of June 1934,
and 'The Battle of Cable Street', in the East End of London, on 4 October
1936. Both appeared to many British people, at the time and later, as
symbols of Fascist brutality and racism.

Mosley gives his account of the Olympia Meeting below:

**3.5**

The peak of organised violence had been reached and surmounted
some years previously in June 1934 at Olympia, a meeting discussed
ever since. There the victory for free speech was not won without
bitter experience. We were not only up against the hooligans

described by Mr. Churchill as 'reptiles' – often armed and under          5
alien instigation – but also the support given to them by more
respectable people.

A collection of weapons taken from the attackers was afterwards
made and the photographs are still on record. Our stewards had to
eject these armed men with their bare hands, for they were not only     10
forbidden to carry weapons but were often searched to ensure the
order was obeyed . . . Were our stewards really to be blamed if they
punched with their fists men who attacked them with 'razors,
knuckle-dusters and iron bars'?

Why then did we find it necessary to organise a dressing-station at     15
Olympia, which we intended to be another political meeting to
convert the British people to our cause, after a series of quiet
meetings which had followed the effective organisation of the
blackshirt movement? The answer is that the attack on the meeting
was openly organised in advance. We knew all about it, and so did       20
the authorities. For three weeks before the meeting, incitements to
attack it were published, and maps were printed to show how to get
to the meeting. For instance on May 17: 'The London District
Committee of the Communist Party has decided to call upon the
London workers to organise a counter-demonstration against the         25
demonstration of Sir Oswald Mosley, which is advertised to take
place at Olympia on Thursday, June 7th'.

**Sir Oswald Mosley,** *My Life*, **Nelson, 1968, pp. 296–7**

A different view of the meeting is given by Philip Toynbee, then an
eighteen-year-old Communist waiting to go up to Oxford:

**3.6**

But the third day provided what I had lacked before, emotional
justification for my escapade. Sir Oswald Mosley held a monster
meeting at Olympia. In the afternoon we bought knuckle-dusters at a
Drury Lane ironmongers, and I well remember the exaltation of
trying them on . . .                                                     5

We seethed with the anti-fascist crowd down the cul-de-sac beside
Addison Road Station, at one moment carrying between us a great
two-poled crimson streamer, dropping it at the next to escape from
the hooves of the mounted police, shouting fierce slogans against the
long, protected column of fascists.                                     10

One – Two – Three – Four!
What – are – the fascists – for?
Lechery, Treachery, Hunger and War.

Later we had somehow contrived to penetrate into the great
auditorium itself. Olympia was nearly full – tier upon tier of the 15
curious and the enthusiastic, and the enthusiastic in great majority.
In every open space, at the end of every row, stood black-jerseyed
stewards with hands on hips, complacent and menacing. The seats
had been full for many minutes before hidden trumpets sounded a
fanfare, and the Leader strode into the arc-lights. He was flanked by 20
four blond young men, and a platoon of flag-bearing blackshirts
following in their wake. The procession moved very slowly down the
aisle, amid shouts, screams and bellows of admiration . . . Sir Oswald
held one arm at his side, thumb in leather belt: the other flapped
nonchalently from time to time as he turned a high chin to inspect 25
us.

   He had stood at the rostrum for at least two minutes in this din,
before his own arm rose, formidably, to impose silence. And then . . .
not the commanding single voice, but a sudden blasphemous
interruption from behind us. It was shocking and incredible, as if a 30
scene had been made at a coronation.

Hitler and Mosley mean hunger and war!
Hitler and Mosley mean hunger and war!

The voices, ragged at the opening, had quickly united in the slogan. 35
Yet after the blare of the trumpets and all the applause, they seemed
lost and thin in the great cavern of the auditorium. I turned just in
time to see three young men and a girl standing side by side, their
mouths open, their alarmed, defiant faces raised towards the ceiling.
A moment later the stewards had closed in on them and they had 40
sunk out of sight in a storm of black bodies and white fists.

**Philip Toynbee, *Friends Apart*, Macgibbon and Kee, 1954, pp. 21–2**

Fenner Brockway, the ILP leader, gives an eye-witness account of 'The
Battle of Cable Street' in 1936:

3.7

The most impressive co-operation between the I.L.P. and the
Communist Party was in opposition to the offensive conducted by Sir

Oswald Mosley and his British Union of Fascists in East London.
Playing on the prejudice against Jews, Mosley had succeeded in
securing the support of a considerable number of Irish and British    5
workers and planned a march through the East End on 4 October
1936. I regarded this as a deliberate racial provocation and co-
operated readily in resistance. Both the I.L.P. and the C.P. held
meetings calling on the workers to mass on the streets to bar the way
of the fascist procession; the idea was that if the streets were      10
crammed the march would have to be abandoned.

I went down to the East End early and joined the crowd at
Gardner's Corner beyond Aldgate. Every moment more people came.
From a balcony the cinema and press photographers took their shots
of the surging masses through whom mounted police tried in vain to    15
force an avenue for the procession. Glass windows crashed as the
weight of the crowd was thrust against shop fronts; the temper of the
police began to rise and they used their batons freely . . . in one
police rush [I] was knocked over and trampled on a little. By now
some among both the police and the crowd were losing their heads.     20
The crowd was jeering provocatively; sometimes the police used their
batons fiercely and with anger in their faces.

Fenner Brockway, *Inside the Left*, Allen and Unwin, 1942, pp. 270–3

## Questions

1    With reference to document **3.4**,
     (i) what major criticisms of the contemporary British economic and
         political system are made by Mosley?
     (ii) what practical changes does he suggest or imply would be
         introduced by the British Fascists if they achieved power?
     (iii) do you detect any continuity between the ideas expressed here
         [**3.4**] and Mosley's earlier attacks on the leadership and policies
         of the second Labour Government [**1.3** and **1.4**]?
     (iv) what sort of people would you expect to be attracted to the
         Fascist creed in the early 1930s?
2    (i) 'We are organised, therefore, as a disciplined army' [**3.4, line
         36**]. What features of the British Union of Fascists illustrate
         this?
     (ii) 'We are essentially a national movement' [**line 16**]. How far was
         this true of the British Union of Fascists?
3    (i) Mosley always protested that he was not anti-Semitic in the

1930s. Is any evidence on this point presented in documents **3.4** to **3.7**?

(ii) Mosley wrote in 1936, 'We are accused of organising to practice violence. That accusation is untrue'. What light is thrown on this assertion by the above documents?

(iii) What action was taken by the government after 'the battle of Cable Street' to deal with the problem of street violence?

4   'The British Fascists were a troublesome nuisance rather than a public danger'. Discuss.

5   With reference to documents **3.2** and **3.3** and documents **3.4** to **3.7**, do you detect any similarities between the British Fascists and Communists in the 1930s from the point of view of

   (i) their analysis of British society and

   (ii) their political methods and aims?

6   'The British Union of Fascists was weakening both in the provinces and in the capital by the late thirties, and it was killed by the war'. Why was this?

# 4  The general election of 1945

By the spring of 1945, with the imminent collapse of Germany, the question of the future of the Churchill Coalition government became of immediate public importance. The problem was in the first place one for the Prime Minister. In the previous year Churchill had indicated that unless there was a real desire by all three political parties to continue the Coalition, then 'we must look to the termination of the war against Nazism as a pointer which will fix the date of the general election'. After the surrender of Germany on 7 May 1945, the realistic choice for Churchill appeared to be between an immediate election or one in October, which would have allowed time for the electoral registers to be brought up to date. His party favoured an early election, hoping to cash in on the Prime Minister's popularity, though Churchill himself favoured continuing the Coalition until the end of the war with Japan. He therefore offered Attlee the choice of an election either immediately or after the defeat of Japan. The Labour Party – then meeting in conference at Blackpool – plumped for an early election. Churchill thereupon resigned on 23 May and formed a 'Caretaker' government until the result of the general election, to be held on 5 July, was known.

Below are some extracts from the Conservative and Labour electoral Manifestos:

4.1

CONSERVATIVE MANIFESTO 1945
Mr Churchill's Declaration of Policy to the Electors

This is the time for freeing energies, not stifling them. Britain's greatness has been built on character and daring, not on docility to a State machine. At all costs we must preserve that spirit of            5
independence and that 'Right to live by no man's leave underneath the law'.

During a whole year of this great war Britain bore the burden of the struggle alone. She must not lose her position in world affairs now that the war in Europe is won. She cannot afford to break and            10 squander the splendid organisms of defence, Naval, Army and Air, which she has with so much effort brought into existence . . .

In the first year of peace, the provision of homes will be the greatest domestic task . . .

National well-being is founded on good employment, good housing and good health. But there always remain those personal hazards of fortune, such as illness, accident or loss of a job, or industrial injury, which may leave the individual and his family unexpectedly in distress. In addition, old age, death and child-birth throw heavy burdens upon the family income.

One of our most important tasks will be to pass into law and bring into action as soon as we can a nation-wide and compulsory scheme of National Insurance based on the plan announced by the Government of all Parties in 1944 . . .

The health services of the country will be made available to all citizens. Everyone will contribute to the cost, and no one will be denied the attention, the treatment or the appliances he requires because he cannot afford them.

We propose to create a comprehensive health service covering the whole range of medical treatment from the general practitioner to the specialist, and from the hospital to convalescence and rehabilitation; and to introduce legislation for this purpose in the new Parliament.

The more efficient British industry is and the fuller use it makes of modern methods and materials, the higher will be the standard of wellbeing that is possible for our people . . . As against the advocates of State ownership and control, we stand for the fullest opportunity for go and push in all ranks throughout the whole nation. This quality is part of the genius of the British people, who mean to be free to use their own judgement and never intend to be State serfs . . . We stand for the removal of all controls as quickly as the need for them disappears . . . We intend to guard the people of this country against those who, under guise of war necessity, would like to impose upon Britain for their own purposes a permanent system of bureaucratic control, reeking of totalitarianism . . .

The small man in trade or industry . . . must be given every chance to make good. His independence of spirit is one of the essential elements that make up the life of a free society.

Coal is owned by the State, and is a wasting asset . . . Wartime measures are not suited to peacetime conditions. A new, practical start is needed . . . A central authority, appointed by the Minister of

15

20

25

30

35

40

45

50

Fuel and subject to his general direction, will be set up, to insist that the necessary measures are taken and to provide such help and guidance as is useful . . .

We are dedicated to the purpose of helping to rebuild Britain on the sure foundations on which her greatness rests. In recent generations, enormous material progress has been made. That progress must be extended and accelerated not by subordinating the individual to the authority of the State, but by providing the conditions in which no one shall be precluded by poverty, ignorance, insecurity, or the selfishness of others from making the best of the gifts with which Providence has endowed him.

Our programme is not based upon unproved theories or fine phrases, but upon principles that have been tested anew in the fires of war and not found wanting. We commend it to the country not as offering an easy road to the nation's goal but because, while safeguarding our ancient liberties, it tackles practical problems in a practical way.

F. W. S. Craig, **British General Election Manifestos 1918–66**, Political Reference Publications, Chichester, 1970, pp. 87–97

**4.2**

## LABOUR MANIFESTO 1945
Let us Face the Future: a Declaration of Labour Policy
for the Consideration of the Nation

So far as Britain's contribution is concerned, this war will have been won by its people, not by any one man or set of men though strong and greatly valued leadership has been given to the high resolve of the people in the present struggle. And in this leadership the Labour Ministers have taken their full share of burdens and responsibilities . . .

What will the Labour Party do?

First, the whole of the national resources in land, material and labour must be fully employed. Production must be raised to the highest level and related to purchasing power . . . Secondly, a high and constant purchasing power can be maintained through good wages, social services and insurance, and taxation which bears less heavily on the lower income groups. But everybody knows that money and savings lose their value if prices rise, so rents and the prices of the necessities of life will be controlled . . .

But a policy of Jobs for All must be associated with a policy of
general economic expansion and efficiency as set out in the next
section of this Declaration . . .                                           20

The Labour Party is a Socialist Party, and proud of it. Its ultimate
purpose at home is the establishment of the Socialist Commonwealth
of Great Britain – free, democratic, efficient, progressive, public-
spirited, its material resources organised in the service of the British
people.                                                                     25

But Socialism cannot come overnight, as the product of a week-end
revolution. The members of the Labour Party, like the British
people, are practical-minded men and women.

There are basic industries ripe and over-ripe for public ownership
and management in the direct service of the nation. There are many         30
smaller businesses rendering good service which can be left to go on
with their useful work.

There are big industries not yet ripe for public ownership which
must nevertheless be required by constructive supervision to further
the nation's needs and not to prejudice national interests by              35
restrictive anti-social monopoly or cartel agreements – caring for their
own capital structures and profits at the cost of a lower standard of
living for all.

In the light of these considerations, the Labour Party submits to
the nation the following industrial programme:                             40
  1 Public ownership of the fuel and power industries . . .
  2 Public ownership of inland transport . . .
  3 Public ownership of iron and steel . . .
  4 Public supervision of monopolies and cartels . . .
  5 A firm and clear-cut programme for the export trade . . .              45
  6 The shaping of suitable economic and price controls to secure
    that first things shall come first in the transition from war to
    peace . . .

Housing will be one of the greatest and one of the earliest tests of a
Government's real determination to put the nation first. Labour's          50
pledge is firm and direct – it will proceed with a housing programme
with the maximum practical speed until every family in this island
has a good standard of accommodation . . .

The best health services should be available for all . . . [through]
the new National Health Service . . . A Labour Government will              55
press on rapidly with legislation extending social insurance over the
necessary wide field to all.

No domestic policy, however wisely framed and courageously
applied, can succeed in a world still threatened by war. Economic
strife and political and military insecurity are enemies of peace. We        60
cannot cut ourselves off from the rest of the world – and we ought
not to try.

F. W. S. Craig, *British General Election Manifestos 1918–66*, Political
Reference Publications, Chichester, 1970, pp. 97–104

## Questions

1    In what ways do the manifestos [4.1 and 4.2] differ from one
another in their appeal to the electorate?

2    Compare the different ways in which the manifestos deal with
(i) foreign policy
(ii) the economy
(iii) social welfare

3    How does the Labour Manifesto of 1945 [4.2] differ from that of
1935 [3.1]?

4    Why, and in what ways, does the Conservative Manifesto [4.1]
reflect a change in attitude on domestic issues, as compared with that
of the pre-war party?

Below are three accounts of the general election of July 1945. The first one
is by Harold Macmillan, then parliamentary candidate for Stockton:

4.3

As soon as electioneering began in earnest I knew what the result
would be. Three weeks of campaigning passed quietly, much too
quietly. My meetings were well attended, but dull and uneventful . . .
we carried through the campaign as best as we could, but I had little
hope of success. Many people believed that Churchill's first speech         5
on the wireless was a turning point to our disadvantage. It was
certainly unbalanced and ill-advised. He prophesied a growing control
of all our lives if the Socialists won. He attributed to the ultimate
realisation of Socialism in Britain the kind of political features that
were associated with the Gestapo. But the use of this terrible word in        10
connection with his opponents was a grievous error. Moreover, it was
easy to deride as an outrage the implied attack on colleagues with
whom he had been working in perfect amity for the last five years –

men of moderate opinions such as Attlee, Morrison and, above all, Bevin . . . at the time it shocked as well as angered ordinary folk. I     15 do not believe, however, that this incident was in any way decisive. The election in my view, was lost before it started.

    Churchill was buoyed up by the enthusiastic reception which he had received in his 1000-mile electoral tour. Vast crowds, who had hardly seen him in person since the beginning of the war and had     20 only heard his voice through those famous broadcasts by which they had been sustained in times of disaster and inspired in moments of success, turned out in flocks to see and applaud him. They wanted to thank him for what he had done for them; and in all that they were sincere. But this did not mean that they wanted to entrust him and     25 his Tory colleagues with the conduct of their lives in the years that were to follow. They had been persuaded, civilians and servicemen alike, during the last years of war, that immediately the struggle was over there would follow a kind of automatic Utopia. The British people would move with hardly an effort into a Socialist or semi-     30 Socialist State under their own leaders, which would bring about unexampled prosperity in a world of universal peace. Nor had they forgotten or been allowed to forget the years before the war. Pamphlets and books attacking the 'guilty men of Munich' were published and circulated in vast numbers. It was not Churchill who     35 lost the 1945 election; it was the ghost of Neville Chamberlain.

**Harold Macmillan, *Tides of Fortune 1945–1955*, Macmillan, 1969, pp. 31–3**

Independent Socialist and writer, George Orwell, describes the election from a different point of view:

4.4

    The anomalies of the English electoral system usually work in favour of the Conservatives, and everyone assumed that they would do so again. Actually they worked the other way, for once, and everyone was stunned with surprise when the results were announced. But I was also wrong in suggesting that the Labour leaders might flinch     5 from power and hence fight the election half-heartedly. It was a genuine enough fight, and it turned on issues that were serious so far as they went. Everyone who took an interest saw that the only chance

of getting the Tories out was to vote Labour, and the minor parties
were ignored. The twenty candidates put up by the Communists only     10
won about 100,000 votes between them, and Commonwealth did
equally badly. I think that the democratic tradition came out of the
election fairly well. Tory efforts to turn the whole thing into a sort of
plebiscite only excited disgust, and though the big masses appeared
uninterested, they did go into the polling booths and vote at the last     15
minute – against Churchill, as it turned out. But one cannot take this
slide to the Left as meaning that Britain is on the verge of revolution.
In spite of the discontent smouldering in the armed forces, the mood
of the country seems to me less revolutionary, less Utopian, even less
hopeful, than it was in 1940 or 1942.     20

**George Orwell, 'London Letter to *Partisan Review*, 15 August 1945',
in *The Collected Essays, Journalism and Letters of George Orwell*,
vol. 3, Penguin Books, 1970, pp. 447–8**

Another parliamentary candidate, Hugh Dalton, who was, incidentally,
standing for a similar constituency to Macmillan – Bishop Auckland in the
North-East of England – gives this account:

**4.5**

In fact, I much over-estimated the P.M.'s personal influence on
votes. The crowds which cheered him on his triumphal tours went
into the polling booths and voted him down. And the soldiers, sailors
and airmen voted overwhelmingly Labour.

As the war in Europe drew towards the end, the P.M., I heard,     5
said to Air Chief Marshal Harris: 'I suppose that, when the election
comes, I can count on the votes of most of the men in the Air
Force?' 'No, sir,' replied Harris, 'eighty per cent of them will vote
Labour.' 'Well at least that will give me twenty per cent', said the
P.M., sharply taken aback. 'No, sir, the other twenty per cent won't     10
vote at all'.

The Laski affair was most irritating, though I don't think it turned
many votes against us . . .

We polled on July 5th . . . Hopes had been rising since the poll,
but I still couldn't persuade myself that we could have won more     15
than 280 seats. Probably, therefore, there would be either a small
Tory majority or a deadlock.

'July 26th, 1945.

| Uneventful count | Result | |
|---|---|---|
| Dalton | 20,100 | 20 |
| Tily | 11,240 | |
| Labour majority | 8,860' | |

Compared with 1935 my majority was up by less than a thousand, though the total vote was down. Taking a line through this, we had clearly not got a Labour majority in the country as a whole. But, while we were waiting for our own result, the news came through that George Chetwynd had won Stockton. At once this lifted hopes sky high. I said to my friends: 'That means we've won the election, and there will be a Labour Government' . . .

The final results of the general election were Labour 396; Tories and Liberal Nationals 213; Liberals 12; Others 19; Labour majority over all 152.

**Hugh Dalton, *The Fateful Years: Memoirs 1931–45*, Muller, Blond and White, 1957, pp. 463–6**

## Questions

1   With reference to document 4.3,
   (i) why did the electorate distinguish between Churchill and the Conservative party?
   (ii) what does 'the Gestapo speech' tell us about Churchill's attitudes during the election campaign?
   (iii) explain and discuss Macmillan's view that 'it was not Churchill who lost the 1945 election; it was the ghost of Neville Chamberlain' [lines 35–36].
2   Why did the 'minor parties' (and especially the Liberals) do so badly in the 1945 election?
3   Compare the views of Macmillan and Orwell [4.3 and 4.4] on why the British people voted Labour. Who is nearer the truth?
4   How do Orwell's views [4.4] reflect on Labour's aims in its Manifesto [4.2]?
5   'Macmillan's later account of the 1945 election is of more value to the historian than Orwell's contemporary description'. Discuss.
6   Why did it prove so difficult to predict accurately the result of the election?

Why did Labour win the 1945 general election? The reasons are directly related to the war-time experience of the British people, since it was then, as Paul Addison has shown, that 'popular opinion swung towards Labour' and gave it its decisive electoral victory[1]. Labour both reflected and helped to create this leftward trend of opinion. One reason for this was the happenings of 1940. Events at Dunkirk, and the new spirit of national unity and social awareness that emerged thereafter, meant that public opinion turned against those held responsible for pre-war unemployment, the policy of Appeasement and the failure to rearm – Baldwin, Chamberlain and the official Conservative Party. Labour, the Opposition party in the 1930s, was bound to gain from this identification, if only by default. The hopes for 'a better world' created by this disillusionment were encouraged by a host of leftish, semi-official propagandists like J. B. Priestley, whose Sunday evening *Postcripts* were heard by millions in the summer of 1940.

**4.6**

Now, there are two ways of looking at this war. The first way, which, on the whole, we are officially encouraged to adopt, is to see this war as a terrible interruption. As soon as we can decently do it, we must return to what is called peace, so let's make all the munitions we can, and be ready to do some hard fighting, and then we can have done       5
with Hitler and his Nazis and go back to where we started from, the day before war was declared. Now this, to my mind, is all wrong. It's wrong because it simply isn't true. A year ago, though we hadn't actually declared war, there wasn't real peace . . .

This brings us to the second, and more truthful, way of looking at      10
this war. That is, to regard this war as one chapter in a tremendous history of a changing world, the breakdown of one vast system and the building up of another and better one . . . There's nothing that really worked that we can go back to . . . But we can't go forward and build up this new world order, and that is our real war aim,        15
unless we begin to think differently, and my own personal view, for what it's worth, is that we must stop thinking in terms of property and power and begin thinking in terms of community and creation . . . And even already, in the middle of this war, I can see that world shaping itself.        20

And now we'll take the change from property to community. Property is that old-fashioned way of thinking of a country as a thing, and a collection of things on that thing, all owned by certain people and constituting property; instead of thinking of a country as the

home of a living society, and considering the welfare of that society,     25
the community itself, as the first test . . . Now, the war, because it
demands a huge collective effort, is compelling us to change not only
our ordinary social and economic habits, but also our habits of
thought. We're actually changing over from the property view to the
sense of community, which simply means we realise we're all in the     30
same boat.

J. B. Priestley, *Postcripts*, Heinemann, 1940, pp. 35–8

Just as important as this change in the 'climate of opinion' in accounting
for a growing pro-Labour sentiment, was the simple fact that, after the
formation of Churchill's Coalition government in 1940, the Home Front
was dominated by 'Labour's Big Three' – Clement Attlee, Ernest Bevin and
Herbert Morrison. They were able to use their key positions to promulgate
their notions of 'planning' and 'egalitarianism' as a vital contribution to
the war effort – especially Bevin as Minister of Labour. At the same time
they could push their ideas on future (and, to some extent, present)
domestic policy through their membership of major government commit-
tees, especially the important Reconstruction Committee.

J. T. Murphy discusses 'Labour's Big Three' below:

**4.7**

The day upon which Attlee, Morrison and Bevin joined the Coalition
Cabinet led by Churchill came amidst the most amazing period of
England's history . . . This time there was no split in the ranks of
Labour . . . Never had the Labour Movement been more unanimous
and determined in its unity to wage the war . . . Behind Attlee,     5
Morrison and Bevin was the united Labour Movement, now
thoroughly roused as everyone became conscious of the overwhelming
power of the enemy and the totally unprepared position of the
country. The 'phoney war' was at an end. Our forces were being
driven into the sea. The political basis for a united nation was     10
established in a struggle for self-existence. Attlee, now Lord Privy
Seal and functioning as deputy Prime Minister, declared to the
House of Commons on May 22nd, 1940: 'The Government demands
complete control over persons and property, not just some persons
and some particular section of the community, but of all persons, rich     15
and poor, employer and work man, men and women, and all

property' . . . The war had created a most desperately popular front.
It had thrust the three Labour leaders into three of the most
important positions in the Government, and for the next five years
they would be compelled, by the very nature of the situation and the      20
jobs they had to tackle, to examine the real relation of social forces,
the real economic and political situation, and to apply certain socialist
principles that were forced by events into the forefront. Every
question would have to be faced from the standpoint of the interests
of the nation as a whole . . . The interests of 'the nation as a whole'      25
is the first principle of socialism . . .

**J. T. Murphy, *Labour's Big Three*, The Bodley Head, 1948, pp. 207–13**

## Questions

1    How would you account for the enormous popularity of Priestley's
     broadcasts? In what ways do his ideas fit in with the ethos of the
     Labour Party?
2    Referring to documents 4.6 and 4.7, what evidence is there to
     suggest that there was a new 'political awareness' and new 'habits of
     thought' among the electorate?
3    Why was Bevin such an outstanding Minister of Labour? In what
     ways did Labour's membership of the Churchill Coalition improve
     the unity, leadership and morale of the Labour Party?

Following Labour's overwhelming victory at the general election, Churchill resigned on 26 July and Attlee accepted the King's commission to
form a new government. The major offices were soon filled. For the first
time in its history the Labour Party had formed an administration which
rested upon an overall majority in the House of Commons.

## References

1   Paul Addison, *The Road to 1945*, Quartet Books, 1977, p. 13

# 5 Clement Attlee and the Labour Party

Clement Attlee was born into an upper-middle class London family in 1883. His father was a solicitor, and he himself was educated at Haileybury and University College, Oxford – institutions to which he remained devoted throughout his life. He was called to the Bar in 1906, but never really practised law. He had already begun a life-long association with the East End of London by working at the Haileybury Boys' Club in Stepney, and it was this contact with the poverty and deprivation of working-class life that turned him to Socialism. In 1908 Attlee joined the Stepney branch of the ILP, and continued his social and political work in the area until he joined the army on the outbreak of war in 1914. After he was demobilised in 1919 as 'Major Attlee', he resumed his association with the East End Labour movement, and was elected a Stepney councillor and soon afterwards Mayor of the borough. In 1922 he was returned as Labour MP for Limehouse. He was encouraged by MacDonald, and given junior office in the 1924 Labour government. He was also appointed a member of the Simon Commission on India, thus becoming one of the few Labour MPs with any practical experience of imperial problems. In 1931 he was made Postmaster-General in the second Labour government, but like the bulk of the Labour Party, he refused to support the formation of the National government.

Unlike most of his parliamentary colleagues, Attlee was lucky enough to retain his seat at the disastrous general election of 1931. As one of the few ex-ministers re-elected, he was appointed deputy to George Lansbury, now party leader. After Lansbury's resignation in 1935, Attlee was put in charge of Labour's campaign in the general election of that year. When parliament re-assembled, he stood against Herbert Morrison and Arthur Greenwood (who had both regained their seats) and was elected leader of the Labour Party.

Douglas Jay, then a young financial journalist, who later served in the 1945 government, describes the leadership contest:

5.1

In the general election of 1935, fought on the issue of Abyssinia and collective security, I joined Gaitskell and Evan Durbin in Chatham

and Gillingham, where respectively they were standing –
unsuccessfully – as Labour candidates . . . In the same year we went
together to a meeting at the Friends' House in Euston Road to hear      5
the result of the election of the new leader of the Labour Party,
following George Lansbury's resignation. The candidates were
Morrison, Attlee and Greenwood. We were all three passionately in
favour of Morrison, who had heartened the whole Party by winning
the LCC election the year before. When we heard that Attlee had        10
won, we three went home filled with deep gloom. To us at this stage
he seemed an unglamorous, routine member of the Parliamentary
Labour Party. How wrong we all were; and what a justification this
election was of the choice of a leader by Members of Parliament only,
who happen to know the man they are selecting! Attlee's rare           15
qualities were never on show, and it took the outside world some
years to perceive what his immediate colleagues had already seen in
1935. But at least one non-MP had spotted them even in that year –
Ernie Bevin. The story is well-known of Bevin's denunciation at the
1935 Party Conference of Lansbury's impractical pacifism. Less well-   20
known is a tale told me forty years later by a member of the
Hampstead Labour Party, Mark Bass, who claimed to have been
present at a meeting at Transport House in 1935. I cannot vouch for
its authenticity; but it struck me as true in spirit. Bevin was
criticising Lansbury, and someone asked him what alternative leader    25
was available. Bevin, pointing at Attlee, replied: 'Do you see that
little man in the corner who smokes a pipe and says nothing? I don't
know much about him. But he'd do.'

**Douglas Jay, *Change and Fortune*, Hutchinson, 1980, pp. 57–8**

On most issues in the 1930s, it is fair to say that Attlee occupied an
uninspiring position between Left and Right. This, together with his
unassuming personality, led to grumbles in 1939 about his lack of
leadership; though, as with all later attempts to displace him, they led
nowhere. It was Attlee, therefore, who took a united Labour Party into
support for the war in September 1939. In the crisis of May 1940 it was the
refusal of Attlee and the Labour Party to serve under Neville Chamberlain,
that enabled Winston Churchill to become Prime Minister and form a new
Coalition government. As a result, prominent Labour politicians like Attlee
himself, Morrison and Bevin, served as members of the new War Cabinet.
The work of Bevin and Morrison as Minister of Labour and Home Secretary

respectively, is well known: the contribution of Attlee was in its way just as decisive.

An *Observer* profile describes the Labour leader in 1944:

**5.2**

At Cabinet meetings the Deputy Prime Minister always sits on the edge of his chair. The trick is typical of the man. It is the sign of a diffidence, a lack of confidence, perhaps better, a modesty, that must be almost unique in high politics.

Yet this is the man, who, on merit, is wartime Number 2 to Mr     5
Churchill of all people. The debt owed to loyal Clem Attlee by the Prime Minister, the country and the Labour Party is big. The post of Deputy Prime Minister was literally made for him and he for it; he fills it without envy.

Outside the Councils of State, too, Mr Attlee is true to type. He is     10
almost anonymous. Slight in figure, he does not stand out in a crowd. Thin in voice, he is at a disadvantage in this Broadcasting Age. He is the forgotten Minister who four years ago brought in the forgotten Bill to put all persons and all property at the nation's disposal.

How is it that he can be called the 'brace' of the Cabinet? Back in     15
the Cabinet room, or at Party meetings, the answer is plainer. Puffing at his pipe, he puts sound points well and simply. He is no colourful figure or champion of stirring causes; he is the impeccable Chairman – at a time when both Cabinet and Party, ill-sorted and on edge, much need a Chairman. Clem Attlee is the honest broker, the good     20
man who came to the aid of his Party. The fact is, the Labour Party distrusts leadership. The case of Ramsay MacDonald frightened it. Nor does anyone, inside or outside the Party, know where it wishes to be led. All that is certain is that the motley group has somehow to be held together. Clem Attlee is neither bigot, doctrinaire, Labour     25
boss, nor careerist. He puts the whole before the parts. He is a Party man, not a partisan . . .

Historians will give Clem Attlee his due, even under the shadow of Churchill, for he, too, in his own way, is equally an English worthy, though not a Great one. But they will also show how his worth to us     30
in our tangled counsels of these days is a reflection of today's discontents and frustrations . . . Clem Attlee is a Fabian; it is an

infinite progress to the Brave New World he believes in. But his faith is at least real; he is a man of character.

*Observer* profile, in Kenneth Harris, *Attlee*, George Weidenfeld and Nicolson, 1982, pp. 232–3

## Questions

1 Why, according to document 5.1, did Clement Attlee win the leadership contest?
2 To what degree does document 5.2 bear out Jay's impression of Attlee as an 'unglamorous, routine member of the Parliamentary Labour Party' [5.1, line 12]?
3 What is meant by describing Attlee as 'the honest broker' in relation to the Labour Party [5.2, line 20]? Why is the description of him as 'a Fabian' particularly apt [line 32]?
4 What strengths and weaknesses as a politician are revealed in the above portraits of Attlee?
5 'The Labour Party distrusts leadership' [5.2, line 21]. Does the recent history of the Labour Party justify this generalisation?

In the election campaign of 1945 Attlee's qualities of moderation and commonsense shone out, particularly in comparison with the rhetoric of Churchill. Following Labour's landslide victory, Churchill resigned on 26 July and Attlee accepted the King's commission to form a new government.

Despite the economic and financial problems that faced the country, the Labour government swiftly pushed ahead with its programme for nationalisation, the re-organisation of the social services and the establishment of the National Health Service. Since the broad principles were agreed upon, the Prime Minister left the details of policy to his ministers.

Years later, in conversation with the journalist, Francis Williams, Attlee summarised what was done.

5.3

*Williams:* Had you a complete working pattern of policy already in mind when you became Prime Minister?

*Attlee:* Certainly. I was definitely determined to go ahead with plans of nationalisation. I expected some trouble over the Bank of England, but it caused no difficulty; rather odd 5

when you think of all the row and trouble there used to
be about it. Cable and Wireless caused no difficulty
either. There was very little difficulty over gas and
electricity – they were fairly well over already. And there
wasn't much with the mines. Transport was much more     10
difficult and iron and steel had not been worked out by
the time we came in.

There were a lot of post-war problems to clear up of
course, but I thought that we must push ahead.
Fundamental nationalisation had to go ahead because it     15
fell in with the planning, the essential planning of the
country. It wasn't just nationalisation for nationalisation's
sake but the policy in which we believed: that
fundamental things – central banking, transport, fuel and
power – must be taken over by the nation as a basis on     20
which the rest of the re-organisation of the country
would depend. It was also obviously essential in the
socialist sphere to drive on towards social security. There
was the Beveridge Report to which all parties were
committed. There was the making of the Health Service     25
and the co-ordination of all the various social services and
the advance in education. All this didn't really, as they
say, brook delay. And then there were the practical things
– housing, largely a matter of working through local
government, and the building of many new factories . . .     30

Williams:     Looking back, do you think the pattern of nationalised
industry you chose, the public corporation not directly
accountable in detail to Parliament, is the best pattern?

Attlee:     On the whole, yes. Of course, we based our ideas on
experience to some extent. Herbert Morrison was very     35
strong on that, learning from the Transport Bill and so
on. And we took the line that these were businesses
which should be run in a businesslike way and it would
be wrong to have perpetual parliamentary interference in
detail. We put that forward and curiously enough it was     40
also stressed by the Tories . . .

Williams:     There was a different criticism from your own side that
still comes up among some workers in the nationalised

industries, that nationalisation ought to have meant a
bigger share in control by the workers.                                    4

*Attlee:*       We tried to get it, I can't say with an awfully good
response. We tried hard to establish more joint
consultation and things of that kind, but not with much
success. A hangover from the past, I'm afraid. Some of
them still had the old feeling of opposition to any                        5
administration. Others frankly said, 'Well, look,
management isn't our job'.

Francis Williams, *A Prime Minister Remembers*, Heinemann, 1961,
pp. 88–9, 92–3

## Questions

1      What evidence does document 5.3 give for the Conservatives having
put up little opposition to the nationalisation programme?
2        (i) Why was the model of the 'public corporation' adopted for the
nationalised industries?
(ii) On what grounds has this model been criticised within the
Labour movement?
(iii) Would you say that Labour's enthusiasm for nationalisation has
been justified in the light of the subsequent history of
nationalised industries?
3      Referring to document 5.3, do you think a strictly contemporary
document is of more value to the historian than the reminiscences of
a politician 'years later'?

While major advances were being made by the Attlee government on the
domestic front, even more momentous decisions were being taken in the
fields of foreign policy and defence. Though he had the constant support of
the Prime Minister and, generally, the Cabinet, British foreign policy
during this period was essentially the work of one man – Ernest Bevin.

Attlee describes the man and his policies:

## 5.4

'If you have a good dog, don't bark yourself' is a good proverb, and
in Mr. Bevin I had an exceptionally good dog . . . The disturbed

international situation was a constant anxiety during the whole of our
period of office and the work of the Foreign Secretary was very
exacting . . . Bevin knew his own mind, was a first-class negotiator      5
and administrator and evoked loyal co-operation from all. He was
very conscious always of the economic issues that underlay so many
international questions and worked in close co-operation with
successive Chancellors of the Exchequer . . .

Our policy was based on support for the United Nations                    10
Organisation and an honest endeavour to work in close harmony with
the United States and with Soviet Russia. Unfortunately, we
experienced opposition everywhere from the latter. The work of the
quadripartite administration in Germany was frustrated constantly by
Russian intransigence, while at U.N.O. the Russian representative         15
soon showed his intention of abusing the Veto.

While this friction with Russia increased we naturally drew closer
to the United States. This was helped by a change in the attitude of
the Administration as they realised what the assumption of
responsibility in world affairs entailed. Many Americans shed their       20
old isolationism and, with it, some of their long-seated prejudice
against Britain as a predatory imperialist power. They were also
disillusioned with Soviet Russia. The two English-speaking countries
began to realise that their close co-operation was essential to world
peace and prosperity. The holding of the Secretaryship of State by        25
General Marshall and by his successor, Dean Acheson, was an
important factor in the promotion of good relations. Perhaps the
decisive event in establishing the new alignment was Marshall Aid. It
was Bevin who, by his quick follow-up of General Marshall's speech,
made it a prime event; no one realised more than he the need to           30
buttress peace by economic reconstruction. When Poland and
Czechoslovakia accepted the idea of Marshall Aid, his hopes for the
integration of Eastern and Western Europe rose high. The
withdrawal of these acceptances at the orders of the Kremlin dashed
this hope. It was, in fact, a declaration of the 'cold war'.              35

The making of the Brussels Treaty and of the Atlantic Pact, which
was the work of Bevin, was a recognition of the fact that before
Russia would consider reasonable relations with the free world there
must be a building up of strength; strength was the only factor which
the Russians considered . . .                                             40

C. R. Attlee, *As it Happened*, Heinemann, 1954, pp. 170–1, 184–5

COME INTO THE GARDEN, CLEM

Cartoon by Vicky, drawn for the *News Chronicle* but unpublished

## Questions

1    What is meant by 'the cold war' [**5.4, line 35**]? What responsibility does Britain bear for its development?
2    'Before Russia would consider reasonable relations with the free world there must be a building up of strength' [**lines 37–39**]. What special project did Attlee authorise in 1947 to improve Britain's military defences? Why was so little known about the project at the time? Was Attlee's decision a wise one?
3    Identify the three figures in document **5.5**. What do you think Vicky is trying to convey about Britain's position in world affairs?
4    Where do you think the cartoonist's sympathies lie?
5    How far do the views on foreign policy expressed in documents **5.4** and **5.5** contradict one another?

The first two years of the Attlee government were a period of remarkable achievement for Labour. In the following years the government was beset by a multitude of problems, and much of the blame was attached, inevitably, to the Prime Minister. In February 1950, after more than four arduous years in power, Attlee decided to opt for an early election. Labour fought largely on its record, and emerged with an overall majority of only five. Hugh Gaitskell considers the election in his diary:

**5.6**

As to the attitude of the electorate, I had no very definite impressions during the campaign. I cannot say, for example, I could detect any great difference in the attitude of the audience from 1945. Perhaps one might say that on the one side they had acquired a sort of additional confidence in the capacity of Labour to govern, and on the other side had accumulated inevitably a collection of grievances against us for the way some aspects of government had affected them.    5

One result of the Election has certainly been the increase in stature of the P.M. He certainly displayed his remarkable political instinct and gift at their very best. He always found the exact words to counter Churchill, and it is generally agreed that his broadcast was outstanding. When one considers that he is normally thought of as a poor broadcaster and a man with no gift for leadership this is rather extraordinary; though of course it is not the first time in British politics this has happened. One thinks of Baldwin as a most recent example. And in the House now the increased stature has given him increased confidence so that his performances in the Debates have been considerable improvements on the last Parliament. I would also say that in the Cabinet his position is a great deal strengthened.    10    15

*The Diary of Hugh Gaitskell 1945–56*, ed. Philip M. Williams, Cape, 1983, pp. 166–8

## Questions

1    Why did Labour lose from the redistribution of seats? What changes in the franchise system had Labour already introduced which probably helped them slightly?

2    What part was played in this election by the issue of nationalisation?

3    'One result of the Election has certainly been the increase in stature of the P.M.' [5.6, line 8]. Does Attlee's record during his second government, 1950–1, confirm this?

4    Is the comparison of Attlee with Baldwin apt [line 15]?

Attlee's second government was an unhappy one. Cripps retired in 1950 and Bevin died in the spring of 1951. The senior ministers who remained were exhausted and ageing. The appointments of Morrison and Gaitskell as Foreign Secretary and Chancellor of the Exchequer respectively, acted, for different reasons, as divisive rather than unifying factors within the Cabinet. At home, little could be done constructively with such a tiny majority. It was foreign affairs, therefore, and the Korean War in particular, which dominated the government's short life. And it was that war which led indirectly to the dispute over the imposition of health charges.

The disputes within the Cabinet over the health charges merely added one more problem to those that faced ministers, at home and abroad, in the summer of 1951. Attlee decided to hold a general election in September. However unfortunate the timing was for Labour, the party fought hard and well, concentrating again on its achievements over welfare, employment, and production, and playing down nationalisation. There was only a small shift in opinion compared with 1950 in the final results – but enough to give the Conservatives a small but decisive victory.

Douglas Jay describes the election:

5.7

It seemed to me at the time that the 1951 election which had such
lasting results, was unnecessary and undesirable from the point of
view of both the country and the Labour Party. Those who
advocated it argued that it was impossible to carry on for another
year with so tiny a majority. My reply to this was that we had been          5
told in February 1950 we could not survive one Finance Bill, and in
fact we had survived two. To launch an election in the autumn of
1951 appeared to me to be choosing nearly the worst possible
moment. As always, I put this strongly to Gaitskell saying that I felt
it amounted to 'abdication'. To my surprise, Gaitskell was not nearly          10
so strongly convinced of this, though he inclined on balance to agree
with me . . . Morrison was opposed to the election, but he was in
Washington. Dalton, on the other hand, favoured it, arguing that if
Labour lost, it would only be by a few seats, and that if we waited
longer, the loss would have been heavier . . . I still believe that the          15
decision was wrong, and that the main motive for it was that senior
Labour ministers, apart from Morrison, after eleven years in high
office, and with Bevin and Cripps both lost to the Government, felt
too exhausted to carry the burden any longer . . .

It was the most fiercely fought, passionate, neck-and-neck,        20
exhausting parliamentary election I ever contested (out of eleven) . . .
But the Labour Party had almost everything in 1951 against it: the
redistribution of seats, the Bevanite quarrel only six months before,
the loss of Bevin and Cripps, the Korean war burden, and the steady
swing back of votes due to the revival of anti-Labour propaganda in        25
the post-1945 press. Even on top of all this, the withdrawal of a large
number of Liberal candidates, as compared with 1950, undoubtedly
favoured the Conservatives . . . In all the circumstances the result
was as surprising as it was ironic. It was indeed a close-run thing . . .
The result was:        30

| *In seats* | | *In votes* | |
|---|---|---|---|
| Conservatives | 321 | Conservatives | 13,717,538 |
| Labour | 295 | Labour | 13,948,605 |
| Liberals | 6 | Liberals | 730,556 |
| Irish Nationalists | 3 | | 35 |

Douglas Jay, *Change and Fortune*, Hutchinson, 1980, pp. 209–77

## Questions

1    Are Jay's arguments opposing the timing of the September 1951
     election convincing **[5.7]**?
2    Why was the election so 'fiercely fought' **[line 20]**? What reveals
     this?
3    How would you list in order of importance the factors given by Jay
     in this document to explain Labour's defeat? Are there any other
     factors which you consider significant?
4    Examine the figures in the table. Who got the most votes? Who got
     the most seats? Comment.
5    What conclusion can be drawn from the electoral statistics in the
     above document, and other evidence, about the character of the
     British party system in the immediate post-war period? Would you
     say that the character of the British party system today is
     fundamentally different?
6    'The Attlee government marked the climax of British democratic
     socialism'. Discuss.

Attlee resigned as Prime Minister on 26 October 1951, and Churchill once
again resumed office. Attlee carried on as leader – while the Left and Right
of the party fought around him – and the Labour Party suffered an even

more ignominious electoral defeat in 1955. He retired in the autumn of that year, and was succeeded as party leader by Hugh Gaitskell. Honoured as Earl Attlee, and respected universally in his retirement, the former Labour Premier lived long enough to witness his party's return to power in 1964 and 1966. He died on 8 October 1967. His ashes were buried in Westminster Abbey, near the memorial to his former colleague and adversary, Winston Churchill.

# 6 Winston Churchill and British politics

If 1931 was a year of crisis in British politics, for Winston Churchill it represented another turning-point in his long and stormy political career. He was now fifty-seven, and had already spent thirty years in politics since he was first elected to the House of Commons in 1900 as Conservative MP for Oldham. From one point of view, his political career since that date had been a dazzling success. Linked with English politics through his family name – and especially the short but brilliant career of his father, Lord Randolph Churchill – he was appointed to his first government post in 1905, when he was just over thirty. During the next quarter of a century he held most of the great offices of state: President of the Board of Trade, Home Secretary, and First Lord of the Admiralty as a Liberal under Asquith; Minister of Munitions and later War Minister in Lloyd George's Coalition government; and Chancellor of the Exchequer as a Conservative in Baldwin's Second Ministry, 1924–9. Only the Foreign Office eluded him – and of course the Premiership – the office on which his ambitions were firmly centred.

Yet from another point of view, Churchill's political career by 1931 was a tragic failure. He was even farther away from the Premiership than ever. Despite his love for 'coalitions' and 'centre parties', he was not included in the National government, and he remained out of office throughout the 1930s – 'an Ishmael in public life'. Why was this? The causes lie deep in Churchill's character and earlier political career. As far back as 1916 Lloyd George had hinted at some of the answers, when he was forced to bow to Conservative pressure and exclude Churchill from his new Coalition government:

6.1

The third ex-Minister who would have been helpful in Council was Mr. Winston Churchill – one of the most remarkable and puzzling enigmas of his time . . . Unhappily, the Tory Ministers . . . were unanimous in their resolve that he should not be a member of the Ministry . . .

5

Why were they so bitter and implacable? His political record
naturally exasperated his old Party. He does nothing by halves, and
when he left it he attacked his old associates and condemned his old
principles with a vigour and a witty scorn which rankled. When War
was declared the national peril constrained all parties into a                    10
temporary truce, in which party ranks and party rancours were for
the time being overlooked or ignored. But Conservatives could not
forgive nor forget Churchill's desertion to their enemies, and his brisk
and deadly firing into their ranks at a moment when their rout had
begun. Had he remained a faithful son of the political household in                15
which he had been brought up, his share in the Dardanelles fiasco
would have been passed over and another sacrifice would have been
offered up to appease the popular anger . . . His mistakes gave
resentful Tories an irresistible opportunity for punishing rank treason
to their party . . .                                                               20
    For days I discussed with one or other of my colleagues Churchill,
his gifts, his shortcomings, his mistakes . . . They admitted that he
was a man of dazzling talents, that he possessed a forceful and a
fascinating personality. They recognised his courage and that he was
an indefatigable worker. But they asked why, in spite of that,                     25
although he had more admirers, he had fewer followers than any
prominent public man in Britain? . . . Churchill had never attracted,
he had certainly never retained, the affection of any section, province
or town. His changes of Party were not entirely responsible for this.
Some of the greatest figures in British political life had ended in a              30
different Party from that in which they commenced their political
career . . . What then was the reason?
    Here was their explanation. His mind was a powerful machine, but
there lay hidden in its material or its make-up some obscure defect
which prevented it from always running true. They could not tell                   35
what it was. When the mechanism went wrong, its very power made
the action disastrous, not only to himself but to the causes in which
he was engaged and the men with whom he was co-operating. That is
why the latter were nervous in his partnership. He had in their
opinion revealed some tragic flaw in the metal . . . They thought of              40
Churchill not as a contribution to the common stock of activities and
ideas in the hour of danger, but as a further danger to be guarded
against.

Lloyd George, *War Memoirs*, Odhams edn, 1938, vol 1, pp. 636–8

The attitude of Labour was no more favourable than that of the Conservatives, as Emanuel Shinwell indicates:

**6.2**

> Nobody in British politics during the early 'twenties inspired more dislike in Labour circles than Winston Churchill. His crowning sin was his fatuous declaration that Labour was unfit to govern . . . In those days criticism of Churchill was the oustanding feature at meetings organised by the Labour Movement. In every market place   5
> Labour propagandists dwelt upon his eccentricities, quoted his fulminations against the Conservative Party when he was a Liberal and sought with impassioned oratory to expose the iniquities of this 'wayward genius'. Regarded as the principal impediment to Labour's progress, he became the target for almost every epithet in the English   10
> language.
>    When I entered Parliament in 1922, Churchill was not a Member. His sensational rejection by the electors of Dundee at the previous Election was hailed with unconcealed delight by the Labour Party throughout the country. This was the year in which a political   15
> transformation caused the return of the largest number of Labour Members . . . ever known. Not less satisfactory was the defeat of Churchill, Labour's most dangerous opponent, and – there were few who would have dared to deny it – the most brilliant of them all.
>    The election of 1924 failed to bear out the promise of 1922 . . .   20
> Meanwhile, Churchill, who had successfully fought Epping, had joined the Baldwin government. His activities as Chancellor of the Exchequer and as the self-appointed defender of the Constitution during the General Strike served to embitter relations still further between him and the Labour Movement.   25

Emanuel Shinwell, 'Churchill as a Political Opponent', in Charles Eade (ed.), *Churchill by his Contemporaries*, Hutchinson, 1953, pp. 75–6

## Questions

1    Why does Shinwell describe Churchill as 'Labour's most dangerous opponent' [6.2, line 18]?
2    Lloyd George suggests that Churchill 'had never attracted, he had certainly never retained, the affection of any section, province or town' [6.1, lines 27–29].

(i)  What evidence of this is there in Churchill's political career as a whole?

(ii) With particular reference to twentieth-century British politics, how important has the possession of sectional and/or local support been in explaining the rise to party leadership of particular politicians?

3    Compare Shinwell's impression of Churchill with that of Lloyd George. Comment.

4    A 'wayward genius'. From the evidence in documents **6.1** and **6.2**, do you think this is an accurate assessment of Churchill?

Churchill is generally seen in the 1930s as the personification of anti-Appeasement – a view which has been encouraged by his own version of events in 'The Gathering Storm', the first volume of his epic *The Second World War*. Yet in the early thirties, his major interest lay not with Europe but with India. His obstinate opposition to any constitutional change in the government of India made him the centre of political controversy at that time.

Apart from India, it was the defence policy of the National government following Hitler's rise to power in Germany that Churchill particularly castigated. By 1938, particularly after the resignation of Eden in February, he became an out-and-out opponent of Chamberlain's policy of Appeasement (see Chapter 2). Churchill's case against Appeasement was summed up in his speech in the House of Commons on 5 October 1938 attacking the Munich Agreement:

**6.3**

I will . . . begin by saying the most unpopular and unwelcome thing.
I will begin by saying what everybody would like to ignore or forget
but which must nevertheless be stated, namely, that we have
sustained a total and unmitigated defeat, and that France has suffered
even more than we have. The utmost that . . . the Prime Minister has      5
been able to secure by all his immense exertions . . . the utmost he
has been able to secure for Czechoslovakia in the matters which were
in dispute has been that the German dictator, instead of snatching
the victuals from the table, has been content to have them served to
him course by course.                                                     10
     The Chancellor of the Exchequer [Sir John Simon] said it was the
first time Herr Hitler had been made to retract – I think that was the

word – in any degree. We really must not waste time after all this
long Debate upon the difference between the positions reached at
Berchtesgaden, at Godesberg and at Munich. They can be very          15
simply epitomised, if the House will permit me to vary the metaphor.
£1 was demanded at the pistol's point. When it was given, £2 were
demanded at the pistol's point. Finally, the dictator consented to take
£1 17s 6d and the rest in promises of goodwill for the future.

What is the remaining position of Czechoslovakia? Not only are       20
they politically mutilated but, economically and financially, they are
in complete confusion. Their banking, their railway arrangements, are
severed and broken, their industries are curtailed, and the movement
of their population is most cruel . . . I venture to think that in future
the Czechoslovak State cannot be maintained as an independent         25
entity. I think you will find that in a period of time which may be
measured by years, but may be measured only by months,
Czechoslovakia will be engulfed in the Nazi regime . . . But we
cannot consider the abandonment and ruin of Czechoslovakia in the
light only of what happened last month. It is the most grievous        30
consequence of what we have done and of what we have left undone
in the last five years – five years of futile good intentions, five years
of eager search for the line of least resistance, five years of
uninterrupted retreat of British power, five years of neglect of our air
defences. Those are the features which I stand here to expose and     35
which marked an improvident stewardship for which Great Britain
and France have dearly to pay. We have been reduced in those years
from a position of security so overwhelming and so unchallengeable
that we never cared to think about it . . . We have been reduced from
a position of safety and power – power to do good, power to be        40
generous to a beaten foe, power to make terms with Germany, power
to give her proper redress for her grievances, power to stop her
arming if we chose . . . – reduced in five years from a position safe
and unchallenged to where we stand now.

When I think of the fair hopes of a long peace which still lay        45
before Europe at the beginning of 1933 when Herr Hitler first
obtained power, and of all the opportunities of arresting the growth
of Nazi power which have been thrown away . . . I cannot believe
that a parallel exists in the whole course of history. So far as this
country is concerned the responsibility must rest with those who have  50
had the undisputed control of our political affairs. They neither
prevented Germany from rearming, nor did they rearm ourselves in

time. They quarrelled with Italy without saving Ethiopia. They
exploited and discredited the vast institution of the League of
Nations and they neglected to make alliances and combinations which  55
might have repaired previous errors, and thus they left us in the hour
of trial without adequate national defence or effective international
security.

*Into Battle: Speeches by the Right Hon. Winston Churchill* ed.
Randolph S. Churchill, Cassell, 1941, pp. 42–7

## Questions

1     Upon what principles was Churchill's opposition to Chamberlain's
      policy of Appeasement based? In what ways did his attitude differ
      from that of anti-Appeasers on the Left?
2     Do you find Churchill's indictment of the foreign and defence
      policies of the National government, 1933–8, convincing [6.3, **lines
      30–44**]?
3     Why did so few Conservatives in the House of Commons follow
      Churchill and abstain in the vote on the Munich Agreement?
4     'I venture to think that in future the Czechoslovak State cannot be
      maintained as an independent entity' [6.3, **line 24**]. In what way was
      Churchill proved correct in March 1939? How was his political
      position in the country affected by that event?

With the outbreak of war on 3 September 1939, Neville Chamberlain
bowed to the inevitable and appointed Churchill to the Admiralty: hence
the famous signal sent throughout the Fleet – 'Winston is Back!'. Just over
eight months later, Churchill became Prime Minister, as he describes,
memorably, at the end of 'The Gathering Storm':

6.4

The morning of the tenth of May dawned[1] . . . At about 10 o'clock
Sir Kingsley Wood came to see me, having just been with the Prime
Minister. He told me that Mr Chamberlain was inclined to feel that
the great battle which had broken upon us made it necessary for him
to remain at his post. Kingsley Wood had told him that, on the          5
contrary, the new crisis made it all the more necessary to have a
National Government, which alone could confront it, and he added
that Mr Chamberlain had accepted this view. At 11 o'clock I was
again summoned to Downing Street by the Prime Minister. There

once more I found Lord Halifax. We took our seats at the table          10
opposite Mr Chamberlain. He told us that he was satisfied that it was
beyond his power to form a National Government. The response he
had received from the Labour leaders left him in no doubt of this.
The question therefore was whom should he advise the King to send
for after his own resignation had been accepted . . . He looked at us          15
both across the table.

I have had many important interviews in my public life, and this
was certainly the most important. Usually I talk a great deal, but on
this occasion I was silent. Mr Chamberlain evidently had in his mind
the stormy scene in the House of Commons two nights before . . . As          20
I remained silent, a very long pause ensued. It certainly seemed
longer than the two minutes which one observes in the
commemorations of Armistice Day. Then at length Halifax spoke. He
said that he felt that his position as a Peer . . . would make it very
difficult for him to discharge the duties of Prime Minister in a war          25
like this . . . He spoke for some minutes in this sense, and by the
time he had finished it was clear that the duty would fall upon me –
had in fact fallen upon me. Then, for the first time I spoke. I said I
would have no communication with either of the Opposition Parties
until I had the King's Commission to form a Government. On this          30
the momentous conversation came to an end . . .

Presently a message arrived summoning me to the Palace at 6
o'clock . . . I was taken immediately to the King. His Majesty
received me most graciously and bade me sit down. He looked at me
searchingly and quizzically for some moments, and then said: 'I          35
suppose you don't know why I have sent for you?'. Adopting his
mood, I replied: 'Sir, I simply couldn't imagine why'. He laughed
and said: 'I want to ask you to form a Government'. I said I would
certainly do so . . . A Government of National character was
obviously inherent in the situation . . . I told the King that I would          40
immediately send for the leaders of the Labour and Liberal Parties,
that I proposed to form a War Cabinet of five or six Ministers, and
that I hoped to let him have at least five names before midnight. On
this I took my leave and returned to the Admiralty.

During these last crowded days of the political crisis my pulse had          45
not quickened at any moment . . . But I cannot conceal from the
reader . . . that as I went to bed at about 3 a.m., I was conscious of a
profound sense of relief. At last I had the authority to give directions
over the whole scene. I felt as if I were walking with destiny, and

that all my past life had been but a preparation for this hour and for     50
this trial.

**Winston S. Churchill, *The Second World War*, vol. 1, 'The Gathering
Storm', Cassell, 1948, pp. 523–7**

## Questions

1    What was 'the stormy scene in the House of Commons two nights
     before', and why was it so important for Churchill [6.4, line 20]?
2    Why did the Labour Party refuse to serve in the Coalition
     government under Chamberlain, but accepted Churchill's leadership?
     Why, in the light of the Conservative majority in the House of
     Commons, was Churchill so generous to the Labour Party in the
     allocation of key posts?
3    What is the significance of Churchill's retention of Chamberlain and
     Halifax in his new Coalition government?
4    'I felt', writes Churchill, '. . . that all my past life had been but a
     preparation for this hour and for this trial' **[line 50]**. In what sense
     was he justified in making this claim?
5    One historian writes, 'the Great Coalition, as Churchill liked to call
     his administration, was to him more a companionship of arms than
     an alliance of political parties'. Discuss.

Politically, Churchill's position as Prime Minister was not an easy one in
the early months, particularly in relation to the Parliamentary Conservative Party. As a national war leader, however, his authority soon became
virtually unassailable, as the derisory votes recorded against the Coalition
government in 'No Confidence' debates reveals. His personal popularity in
the House of Commons nevertheless varied very much with the fortunes of
war, as 'Chips' Channon records:

**6.5**

29 January 1942

I went to the House; the Lords' Chamber, which we continue to
occupy, was packed. Half a hundred members had to stand; the
Prime Minister was already speaking and again he held the vast
audience enthralled. He was conciliatory, tactful – and, finally,     5
successful. He spoke for 42 minutes and after glancing at the clock
sat down. The Speaker, in his tired voice, put the question twice and

called a division. The Aye Lobby . . . was at once so crowded that
many of the Members were forced to wait in the Chamber . . . When
at last the figures were announced – 464 to 1 – there was a faint  10
cheer. The victory is a triumph for Winston, though there was no
alternative and he knows it. Nevertheless, he is the most inspiring
leader we have . . .

17 February

The House of Commons was restless, crowded and angry, yet it does  15
not seem to know its own mind . . . The PM came into the Chamber
and I saw him scowl. No cheer greeted him as he arrived. Nor as he
answered questions. He seemed to have 'Lost the House'. Then at
twelve o'clock he rose and in a curiously nonchalant, indeed
uninterested, manner, read a prepared statement about the passing  20
through the Channel Straits of the German ships. He convinced
nobody, and particularly his attempt to turn an inglorious defeat into
a victory displeased the House. There was soon a barrage of
questions. Several times the PM intervened and each time his
reception was increasingly hostile; never have I known the House  25
growl at a Prime Minister. Can he ever recover his waning prestige? .
. . he basks only in approval; smiles and praise encourage him;
criticism irritates and restricts him. Today the august assembly nearly
blew up; he was only saved by several dull speakers who so bored the
House . . . that Members began to file out in dozens. It was a  30
disgraceful scene which lasted an hour and there was no dignity or
force; all sense of reality seemed to have left the elected
representatives of the people. We have the first dictator since
Cromwell, and much as I distrust Winston . . . I have even less faith
in the Commons – a more moribund collection of old fogies and nit-  35
wits I have never met.

*Chips: the Diaries of Sir Henry Channon*, ed. R. R. James, George
Weidenfeld and Nicolson, 1967, pp. 319, 322

## Questions

1  (i)  What incident is referred to in 'the passing through the Channel
        Straits of the German ships' [6.5, line 21]?
   (ii) What other major military and naval disasters for Britain had
        already occurred in the winter of 1941–42?

2       What does document **6.5** tell you about Churchill's handling of the
        House of Commons?
3       Can Churchill rightly be described as 'a dictator' during the war
        [**line 33**]? What justification did Channon's contempt for the House
        of Commons have at this time?
4       'Can he ever recover his waning prestige?' [**line 26**]. What military
        events in the latter part of 1942 helped to restore Churchill's
        prestige?
5       'History set him the job that he was the ideal man to do' (Attlee). In
        what ways was Churchill the ideal man as war leader?

With the 'turning of the tide' in the autumn of 1942, Churchill's
dominance and the unity of the Coalition government remained
unimpaired until the end of the European war came in sight in the spring of
1945. As we have already seen in Chapter 4, the defeat of Germany was
followed by the break-up of the Coalition, the general election of July 1945,
and the triumph of Labour.
    Inevitably, the years after 1945 were a period of anti-climax for
Churchill after the dramatic and exhilarating experience of war-time
leadership. Despite his bitter disappointment over the ingratitude of the
electorate, he was determined to carry on as leader of the Opposition.
Despite occasional grumbling within the Parliamentary Conservative
Party, no one was prepared to challenge his claim. Though Churchill had
little positive to offer his supporters in the field of domestic policy, he did
accept, implicitly at least, the need for re-organisation and re-thinking
within the Conservative Party.
    His position and outlook at this time are well described by R. A. Butler,
one of the leaders of the Tory reformers:

**6.6**

        The government's stock in the country remained obstinately high . . .
        But this strength was reinforced by the magnitude and difficulty of
        our own Conservative predicament – our need to convince a broad
        spectrum of the electorate, whose minds were scarred by inter-war
        memories and myths, that we had an alternative policy to Socialism        5
        which was viable, efficient and humane, which would release and
        reward enterprise and initiative but without abandoning social justice
        or reverting to mass unemployment . . .
            It was by no means easy to convince Churchill of this. Defeat had
        not shaken his personal prestige: he had taken it with impressive      1●

dignity and a characteristic stoutness of heart. When he first walked
into the Chamber at the beginning of the new Parliament the
Conservative ranks stood as one man and sang in a deafening roar
'For he's a jolly good fellow'. In active politics as in the hunting
pack, the strongest wolf will retain leadership while his fangs are still      15
firmly bedded in his jaw. It became clear after endless armchair
exchanges that Churchill was fitter than for several years and was
prepared to fight. But the constructive part of his mind always dwelt
more naturally on the international scene than on bread and butter
politics. The themes of Anglo-American partnership and European      20
unity, which he first developed in great speeches at Fulton and
Strasbourg, were of enduring importance . . . They represented a
fitting contribution from a leader of his world fame and stature and
gave him a welcome release from the confinement of domestic
Opposition. On the home front he preferred to employ his formidable      25
powers of exposition and debate to combat what he called 'positive
folly' rather than to propound what I was merely the first of an
increasing number of his colleagues to tell him was necessary, namely
positive policy. This preference of Churchill's was partly
temperamental. But it stemmed also from his historical sense – a wish      30
not to appear . . . peddling nostrums in order to regain power . . .
Honourable as these considerations were, an apter historical analogy
outweighed them. Quintin Hogg put this most pithily when he wrote
to me at the time to say that what the Conservative party needed was
a new Tamworth Manifesto . . .      35
    The 1946 party conference at Blackpool had overwhelmingly
demanded some reformulation of our policy, and Churchill moved to
meet this demand soon after by appointing a special Industrial Policy
Committee . . . I was made Chairman . . . The *Industrial Charter*
neared completion in the early months of 1947 . . .      40

*The Art of the Possible: the Memoirs of Lord Butler*, **Penguin Books,
1973, pp. 134–5, 137, 147–8**

## Questions

1    Examine the reasons given in document **6.6** for the Conservatives'
     defeat in the 1945 election.
2    What *was* the Conservative 'predicament' after 1945 **[line 3]**?
3    What electoral evidence after 1945 showed that 'the government's
     stock in the country remained obstinately high' **[line 1]**?

4       '. . . his mind always dwelt more naturally on the international scene
        than on bread and butter politics' [lines 18–19]. Was this a strength
        or a weakness? Use the documents in this chapter to answer.
5       How appropriate do you find Butler's image of the wolf and 'hunting
        pack' [line 15] in describing the Tory Party after 1945?
6       What points are being made by the Tory reformers in their reference
        to the need for 'a new Tamworth Manifesto' [line 35]?
7       What light is cast on the effectiveness or otherwise of the work of
        Tory reform after 1945 by the election results of 1950 and 1951?

Churchill played a less prominent part, and was more circumspect, in the
elections of 1950 and 1951 than in 1945. His peace-time ministry, which
lasted from October 1951 until he retired in April 1955 when he was
eighty, was personally impressive for a man of his age, but its policies were
unspectacular. This could certainly not be said of the foreign policy of his
successor, Sir Anthony Eden! Churchill (now Sir Winston) was returned
with comfortable majorities at the general elections of 1955 and 1959. But
he was now virtually 'above politics': his only important contribution to
his party during these declining years was to recommend Macmillan
rather than Butler as Eden's successor, after the latter's break-down
following the Suez debacle in 1956. Sir Winston paid his last visit to the
House of Commons – which he had first entered as a young MP when Lord
Salisbury was Prime Minister – in July 1964. He died in January 1965, at
the beginning of the 'Wilson Era'. 'The saviour of his country' (as A. J. P.
Taylor called him), he received a State funeral. At his own request, he was
buried in the village of Bladon, near Woodstock in Oxfordshire, alongside
his parents. As he had always insisted, it was his father, Lord Randolph, the
apostle of 'Tory Democracy', who was his greatest inspiration in politics.

## References

1       As A. J. P. Taylor points out in *English History 1914–45*, OUP 1965, p. 473,
        the famous meeting between Churchill, Halifax and Chamberlain described
        here actually took place on the afternoon of 9 May.

# Index